Joyce Appleby on *Thomas Jefferson*
Louis Auchincloss on *Theodore Roosevelt*
Jean H. Baker on *James Buchanan*
H. W. Brands on *Woodrow Wilson*
Alan Brinkley on *John F. Kennedy*
Douglas Brinkley on *Gerald Ford*
Josiah Bunting III on *Ulysses S. Grant*
James MacGregor Burns and Susan Dunn on *George Washington*
Charles W. Calhoun on *Benjamin Harrison*
Gail Collins on *William Henry Harrison*
Robert Dallek on *Harry S. Truman*
John W. Dean on *Warren G. Harding*
John Patrick Diggins on *John Adams*
Elizabeth Drew on *Richard M. Nixon*
John S. D. Eisenhower on *Zachary Taylor*
Annette Gordon-Reed on *Andrew Johnson*
Henry F. Graff on *Grover Cleveland*
David Greenberg on *Calvin Coolidge*
Gary Hart on *James Monroe*
Hendrik Hertzberg on *Jimmy Carter*
Roy Jenkins on *Franklin Delano Roosevelt*
Zachary Karabell on *Chester Alan Arthur*
Lewis H. Lapham on *William Howard Taft*
William E. Leuchtenburg on *Herbert Hoover*
Gary May on *John Tyler*
George S. McGovern on *Abraham Lincoln*
Timothy Naftali on *George H. W. Bush*
Charles Peters on *Lyndon B. Johnson*
Kevin Phillips on *William McKinley*
Robert V. Remini on *John Quincy Adams*
Ira Rutkow on *James A. Garfield*
John Seigenthaler on *James K. Polk*
Hans L. Trefousse on *Rutherford B. Hayes*
Tom Wicker on *Dwight D. Eisenhower*
Ted Widmer on *Martin Van Buren*
Sean Wilentz on *Andrew Jackson*
Garry Wills on *James Madison*
Julian Zelizer on *Jimmy Carter*

James K. Polk

John Seigenthaler

James K. Polk

THE AMERICAN PRESIDENTS

ARTHUR M. SCHLESINGER, JR., GENERAL EDITOR

Times Books

HENRY HOLT AND COMPANY, NEW YORK

Times Books
Henry Holt and Company, LLC
Publishers since 1866
175 Fifth Avenue
New York, New York 10010
www.henryholt.com

Frontispiece: James K. Polk (1795–1849), 11th President
of the U.S. Undated engraving © Bettmann / CORBIS

Library of Congress Cataloging-in-Publication Data

Seigenthaler, John, 1927–
    James K. Polk / John Seigenthaler.—1st ed.
      p.   cm.—(The American presidents series)
    Includes bibliographical references and index.
    ISBN-13: 978-0-8050-6942-6
    ISBN-10: 0-8050-6942-9
     1. Polk, James K. (James Knox), 1795–1849.   2. Presidents—United States—
Biography.   I. Title.   II. American presidents series (Times Books (Firm))
E417.S38 2004
973.6'1'092—dc21
[B]   2003056368

First Edition 2004

Printed in the United States of America
7 9 10 8

To Jack Seigenthaler

Contents

———

Editor's Note   xiii

Introduction: The Born-Again President   1

1. The Bent Twig   10

2. Old and Young Hickory   27

3. Defender of the Faith   43

4. Another Bargain   70

5. Measures of a Great President   102

6. War   131

7. Polk at Peace   151

Notes   157

Milestones   168

Selected Bibliography   173

Acknowledgments   178

Index   180

Editor's Note

THE AMERICAN PRESIDENCY

The president is the central player in the American political order. That would seem to contradict the intentions of the Founding Fathers. Remembering the horrid example of the British monarchy, they invented a separation of powers in order, as Justice Brandeis later put it, "to preclude the exercise of arbitrary power." Accordingly, they divided the government into three allegedly equal and coordinate branches—the executive, the legislative, and the judiciary.

But a system based on the tripartite separation of powers has an inherent tendency toward inertia and stalemate. One of the three branches must take the initiative if the system is to move. The executive branch alone is structurally capable of taking that initiative. The Founders must have sensed this when they accepted Alexander Hamilton's proposition in the Seventieth Federalist that "energy in the executive is a leading character in the definition of good government." They thus envisaged a strong president—but within an equally strong system of constitutional accountability. (The term *imperial presidency* arose in the 1970s to describe the situation when the balance between power and accountability is upset in favor of the executive.)

The American system of self-government thus comes to focus in the presidency—"the vital place of action in the system," as

Woodrow Wilson put it. Henry Adams, himself the great-grandson and grandson of presidents as well as the most brilliant of American historians, said that the American president "resembles the commander of a ship at sea. He must have a helm to grasp, a course to steer, a port to seek." The men in the White House (thus far only men, alas) in steering their chosen courses have shaped our destiny as a nation.

Biography offers an easy education in American history, rendering the past more human, more vivid, more intimate, more accessible, more connected to ourselves. Biography reminds us that presidents are not supermen. They are human beings too, worrying about decisions, attending to wives and children, juggling balls in the air, and putting on their pants one leg at a time. Indeed, as Emerson contended, "There is properly no history; only biography."

Presidents serve us as inspirations, and they also serve us as warnings. They provide bad examples as well as good. The nation, the Supreme Court has said, has "no right to expect that it will always have wise and humane rulers, sincerely attached to the principles of the Constitution. Wicked men, ambitious of power, with hatred of liberty and contempt of law, may fill the place once occupied by Washington and Lincoln."

The men in the White House express the ideals and the values, the frailties and the flaws, of the voters who send them there. It is altogether natural that we should want to know more about the virtues and the vices of the fellows we have elected to govern us. As we know more about them, we will know more about ourselves. The French political philosopher Joseph de Maistre said, "Every nation has the government it deserves."

At the start of the twenty-first century, forty-two men have made it to the Oval Office. (George W. Bush is counted our forty-third president, because Grover Cleveland, who served nonconsecutive terms, is counted twice.) Of the parade of presidents, a dozen or so lead the polls periodically conducted by historians and political scientists. What makes a great president?

Great presidents possess, or are possessed by, a vision of an ideal America. Their passion, as they grasp the helm, is to set the ship of state on the right course toward the port they seek. Great presidents also have a deep psychic connection with the needs, anxieties, dreams of people. "I do not believe," said Wilson, "that any man can lead who does not act . . . under the impulse of a profound sympathy with those whom he leads—a sympathy which is insight—an insight which is of the heart rather than of the intellect."

"All of our great presidents," said Franklin D. Roosevelt, "were leaders of thought at a time when certain ideas in the life of the nation had to be clarified." So Washington incarnated the idea of federal union, Jefferson and Jackson the idea of democracy, Lincoln union and freedom, Cleveland rugged honesty. Theodore Roosevelt and Wilson, said FDR, were both "moral leaders, each in his own way and his own time, who used the presidency as a pulpit."

To succeed, presidents must not only have a port to seek but they must convince Congress and the electorate that it is a port worth seeking. Politics in a democracy is ultimately an educational process, an adventure in persuasion and consent. Every president stands in Theodore Roosevelt's bully pulpit.

The greatest presidents in the scholars' rankings, Washington, Lincoln, and Franklin Roosevelt, were leaders who confronted and overcame the republic's greatest crises. Crisis widens presidential opportunities for bold and imaginative action. But it does not guarantee presidential greatness. The crisis of secession did not spur Buchanan or the crisis of depression spur Hoover to creative leadership. Their inadequacies in the face of crisis allowed Lincoln and the second Roosevelt to show the difference individuals make to history. Still, even in the absence of first-order crisis, forceful and persuasive presidents—Jefferson, Jackson, James K. Polk, Theodore Roosevelt, Harry Truman, John F. Kennedy, Ronald Reagan, George W. Bush—are able to impose their own priorities on the country.

The diverse drama of the presidency offers a fascinating set of tales. Biographies of American presidents constitute a chronicle of wisdom and folly, nobility and pettiness, courage and cunning, forthrightness and deceit, quarrel and consensus. The turmoil perennially swirling around the White House illuminates the heart of the American democracy.

It is the aim of the American Presidents series to present the grand panorama of our chief executives in volumes compact enough for the busy reader, lucid enough for the student, authoritative enough for the scholar. Each volume offers a distillation of character and career. I hope that these lives will give readers some understanding of the pitfalls and potentialities of the presidency and also of the responsibilities of citizenship. Truman's famous sign—"The buck stops here"—tells only half the story. Citizens cannot escape the ultimate responsibility. It is in the voting booth, not on the presidential desk, that the buck finally stops.

—Arthur M. Schlesinger, Jr.

James K. Polk

Introduction:
The Born-Again President

If Walter Lippmann was right, that all successful democratic politicians are insecure and intimidated, James Knox Polk may be the clear exception. From early adulthood until his death at age fifty-three, just three months after the end of his presidency, Polk was a politician who, however wrong or however challenged, never seemed in doubt. On the first day when he strode onto the floor of the Tennessee House of Representatives, there was about him a moral certitude and self-righteousness that he carried to the White House and that remained with him even as he left it, a worn and sickly man.

Somehow he is the least acknowledged among our presidents of great achievement, which is somewhat mystifying. He boldly exerted the influence of the presidency in both foreign and domestic affairs. He threatened war with the British to take from them a major share of the Oregon Territory, waged war against Mexico to grab California and New Mexico, and increased the landmass of the country by a third, creating a continental nation that reached from ocean to ocean. He reduced the tariff, permanently stripped public tax funds from the unaccountable and often corrupt control of private banks, and created an independent Treasury that was viable for more than sixty years. In the nineteenth century, only Thomas Jefferson, Andrew Jackson, and

Abraham Lincoln would wield the power of the office of chief magistrate as effectively.

His presidency was studded, then, with solid accomplishments and should have attracted recognition, sandwiched as it was between the nation's only two Whig administrations—both of which were listless and interrupted by presidential death and succession. By any analytical standard and by every historian's poll, Polk belongs in the pantheon of near-great presidents. James David Barber in *The Presidential Character* writes:

> The president is not some shapeless organism in a flood of novelties. The pathetic hope that the White House will turn a Caligula into a Marcus Aurelius is as naïve as the fear that ultimate power inevitably corrupts. The problem is to understand . . . what in the personal past foreshadows the presidential future.[1]

Great leaders, and especially great and near-great presidents, make critical decisions and take consequential actions guided by traits of character shaped and molded during a lifetime of change and challenge.

Yet over a career that ran more than a quarter century, as state legislator, U.S. congressman, Speaker of the House, governor, and president, Polk seemed to grow or change little at all. He knew what he knew about traditional Republican orthodoxy, satisfied that he was true to his beliefs, and thus concluded he was indisputably right.

True enough, he learned from his own mistakes (rarely admitting them) as well as from those of others, particularly his mentor and role model, Andrew Jackson. But rather than broadening and liberalizing his vision, his errors seemed to narrow and rigidify his outlook on politics and on life. He was virtually the same intense, partisan, humorless, driven politician at twenty-six that he was at fifty-three.

Still this leader, so lacking in imagination, curiosity, and creativity, dramatically transformed the character and geography of the country.

Had you asked James Knox Polk about his aspirations to become president of the United States a month before the 1844 Democratic National Convention, he would have scorned the question as a mocking insult.

Yes, he envisioned becoming president—someday. Yes, he had dreamed of carrying on the great tradition of his mentor, friend, and hero, Andrew Jackson. And yes, he and Jackson had worked hard over the preceding two years to position Polk to run this year for vice president on the Democratic ticket with former president Martin Van Buren. They were confident that the vice presidency would position Polk to succeed Van Buren as the nation's twelfth president. But the vision had been shattered; the dream had become a nightmare; the hard work wasted. As the party delegates planned to travel that year to the Baltimore convention, many thought of James Knox Polk as a washed-up politician—and Van Buren had made it clear he no longer was looking to Tennessee for his running mate.

Polk, zealous Jacksonian Democrat, twice elected Speaker of the U.S. House of Representatives, immediate past governor of Tennessee, was lost. In August 1843 Tennessee voters had rejected him for a second successive time in his bid to reclaim the governorship of his home state from the Whigs. The floor of the political platform on which he had stood for all his years in public life had collapsed with the suddenness of a hangman's trapdoor. James Knox Polk was politically dead.

Beyond the personal mortification he felt over his defeat, the loss to the Whigs was doubly galling because it dealt a distressing emotional blow to Jackson, aging and ill at the Hermitage, his stately home outside Nashville. Jackson had counted on Polk to revive the flagging fortunes of what he proudly called "the

Democracy" in Tennessee and nationally. Young Hickory, as Polk later would be nicknamed, knew he had failed not just himself but also his idol and their cause.

For many months, Polk and Jackson had strategized to help Martin Van Buren recapture the White House he had lost four years earlier to the first Whig president, William Henry Harrison. The loss had been all the more galling for Democrats when Harrison came down with pneumonia on Inauguration Day and died thirty-one days later. The Whigs had picked John Tyler, a turncoat Democrat from Virginia, as Harrison's vice president in order to give their 1840 ticket regional appeal. It worked. But soon after Tyler became the first vice president in history to take over the presidency because of an incumbent's death, he reverted to many of his Democratic ways. By the 1844 election campaign, the ambitious Whigs had decided to dump their apostate president.

They turned, not surprisingly, to Henry Clay. Captain Whig himself, the founder of the party, would make a third race for the presidency, and he convinced them that 1844 would produce the proverbial charm. President Tyler flirted with the idea of converting back to a Democrat, but party leaders, including Jackson, had no interest in him. Instead Democratic power brokers began to push Van Buren as the man to win back the White House he had lost to Harrison and Tyler. Jackson actively threw his support to the New Yorker. Polk naturally and ambitiously went along.

Jackson's body was decrepit, but his mind and his instincts remained razor sharp. Some Democrats viewed Van Buren and Polk as a weak ticket: one had lost the presidency, and the other had twice lost the governorship of his state. Not Old Hickory. Their abiding loyalty to him was a saving virtue, surpassing all others. It was more than blind loyalty, however. Jackson theorized that a Van Buren–Polk ticket merged moderate and moderate, northerner and southerner, New Yorker and Tennessean into a winning alliance. It was, the frail and failing old man was sure, a team to carry the country against the Whigs and Henry Clay.

The mere thought of Clay, the Great Compromiser, in the White House was enough to put Jackson into paroxysms of emotional distress. He despised Henry Clay. Over the long span of his public life he had made many enemies, but he reserved his most purposeful enmity for the Kentuckian. It was a hatred grounded in politics, but transcended that. It was personal. And bitter. And gnawing.

For one thing, Jackson suspected, despite Clay's denials, that he had been the manipulative force behind a series of newspaper articles published during the 1828 presidential campaign exposing the secret that Jackson and his beloved Rachel had lived in a bigamous, adulterous relationship early in their marriage. The muckraking had snuffed out Rachel's will to live, Jackson believed, and she died before they were able to make the celebrative victory trip to his Washington inaugural.

Before that there had been the "corrupt bargain" struck by Clay with John Quincy Adams following the fractious 1824 presidential campaign. In Jackson's mind, that tainted transaction had robbed him of the president's chair.

Polk, newly elected to office as a state legislator, campaigned at home for Jackson against his three opponents, Secretary of State John Quincy Adams, Secretary of the Treasury William H. Crawford, and House Speaker Henry Clay. The nation voted for Jackson by a large margin, but he failed to get the necessary majority of electoral votes. That meant the House of Representatives would select the president.

Clay, because he ran last in the election, was disqualified as a candidate—but by no means was he powerless. The Speaker met privately with Adams, then used his influence to deliver him the deciding margin of electoral votes from Louisiana, Missouri, Ohio—and his home state of Kentucky, where Adams had not received a single popular vote. It was an audacious move. Clay ignored a specific directive from his own state's legislature to support Jackson over Adams and Crawford. President Adams promptly presented Clay with his reward: the top cabinet office, secretary of state.

With Clay very little was personal in politics. He coveted the presidency, and he was keenly aware that the secretary of state's post was the perfect perch from which to fly to the White House. Four past presidents—Jefferson, Madison, Monroe, and now Adams—had made that flight. And so Clay, the Great Compromiser, cut the deal that undermined popular will.

To Jackson it was more than a deal. The corrupt bargain was a quid pro quo that metastasized into a national scandal. As most voters saw it, the highest office, the presidency, had been traded for the highest cabinet office, secretary of state. Adams and Clay together represented "a Monstrous Union,"[2] cried a South Carolina congressman.

From the distance of Tennessee, James K. Polk, soon to be a member of the U.S. House of Representatives, saw it that way too. A travesty. Disillusioning. Disheartening. Disgraceful. Polk, who had worked hard for Jackson's election, went to Congress in 1825 a wiser and more sober young man. For him the atmosphere in Washington was polluted. He opposed every initiative Adams and Clay undertook. And when Jackson and the voters turned Adams out of office in 1828, Polk was satisfied that he had played a part in a political morality play that had righted a grievous wrong. For the rest of his public life, Polk remembered 1824 as the worst of times and looked thereafter on all his political opponents with a jaundiced eye.

Two decades later, as the election of 1844 approached, Jackson's vision of a Democratic government was fading. Once the Whigs had won the White House in 1840, there was no leader to champion his platform: his war against a national bank; his battle against high tariffs; his struggle for economic justice on behalf of "the planter, the farmer, the mechanic and the laborer"; his dream of expanding the nation westward and preserving the Union.[3] He saw a glimmer of hope for it if the Democrats nominated a ticket of Martin Van Buren and James K. Polk.

The Democratic party, however, was changing, and so were its leaders. Van Buren was running to win the Democratic nomination—for himself. His candidacy was on track. If Polk could not carry Tennessee as a gubernatorial candidate, in 1841 or 1843, how could he possibly help deliver the state to Van Buren's presidential hopes in 1844? Van Buren was indebted to Jackson. Old Hickory had made him vice president in 1833 and guided him to the presidency in 1837. But Polk's loyalty to Jackson and Jackson's dream of the future meant little to him in the political climate of 1844.

A few weeks after his second gubernatorial defeat, Polk wrote Van Buren a stiff-upper-lip letter reporting that he had lost Tennessee because of local matters, but that his state would support the Democrats in the coming presidential contest. A second letter in November 1843 included a weak explanation as to why the Tennessee party convention had decided to send an uninstructed delegation, rather than one committed to Van Buren, to the coming Baltimore convention. Not to worry, he said. Twelve of the thirteen Tennessee delegates would support Van Buren.

Polk offered a closing palliative: the state would go for the Democrats against the Whigs, he predicted, if there was "proper discretion and harmony" demonstrated when the party nominated its candidates.[4] "Proper discretion" was transparent. It meant "if you and I are the nominees." Van Buren was too clever to fall for that. He told Francis Blair, the party editor and power broker, that his fortunes in Tennessee "ha[d] been badly managed."[5] Two days after Christmas, with a pithy, pointed letter, the former president gave the failed former governor the bad news in two words. His reaction to Polk's defeat in Tennessee: "Mortifying and incomprehensible."[6] Everywhere else in the nation Democrats were winning except in the home state of the Democracy, the place that in years past "knew not Federalism." In time, he hoped, Polk would remedy the situation so that "the Old Chief should not go out of the world with his favorite Tennessee in Whig hands."[7]

With receipt of that blunt notice, Polk had to know that not even a passionate deathbed plea from Jackson would move Van Buren to favor him for vice president. Strangely, stubbornly, he refused to withdraw his name from vice presidential consideration as the Baltimore convention neared. Perhaps it was pride or the remote hope that a time might come when his candidacy would serve him or Jackson as some bargaining chip in national party affairs. At the same time, standing in the dark shadows of a second defeat, Polk understood that his political career was, indeed, dashed.

And then the impossible occurred. The bizarre circumstances that propelled James Knox Polk suddenly from the desperate throes of defeat and despair into the White House were as astonishing as a clap of thunder in a clear sky. It was a monumental campaign blunder shared by two wise and seasoned politicians. On the same day, April 26, 1844, Democrat Van Buren and Whig Clay issued strikingly similar statements in two competing Washington newspapers declaring their strong opposition to the early annexation of the independent Republic of Texas as part of the United States.

It was a seminal moment in the history of the United States. These two premier politicians, one or the other destined at that moment to become the next president, abysmally misread national public sentiment and simultaneously adopted a flawed and fatal political strategy. Texas was part of the fiber of the country; Texans were citizens exiled only by temporary circumstance. It had been but eight years since the shocking slaughter by the Mexican army of the brave men at the Alamo and at Goliad. Who in the twenty-six states did not have kin or friends who were Texans? Indeed, the president of the fledgling republic was Sam Houston, the former Tennessee governor, yet another Jackson protégé. In the view of most Americans the invisible line that separated Texas from the

United States was a temporary demarcation, already erased from the minds of most people who lived east of the Mississippi. The time had now come to eradicate it from the maps of the continent. That is what the people thought—but that is what Van Buren and Clay now declared they were against.

Jackson understood at once what the two candidates did not. They had cut their political throats. Immediately, the anesthetized hopes of James K. Polk, under Jackson's guidance, were resuscitated. He was thrust into the Democratic nomination at the Baltimore convention. On Election Day, he surged into office as the eleventh, and the youngest, president of the United States.

1

The Bent Twig

Where did they come from, the conflicted character traits that combined to make James K. Polk less than a natural leader, yet justifiably judged among presidents of great achievement?

Edward Cook, whose *Life of Florence Nightingale* helped illuminate for the world the heroine of the Crimean War, warned biographers about the "natural temptation" to draw too heavily on youthful experiences in explaining the adult. So often, he admonished, writers "magnify some childish incident as prophetic of what is to come thereafter."[1] The child, after all, is not in all things father to the man.

True enough. Nonetheless, Polk's early life offers fascinating clues that perhaps help explain the development of a president with the missionary zeal of a fundamentalist preacher determined to convert the populace to Jackson's Democracy. Polk's oratory fell somewhat short of evangelistic eloquence, but his religion was partisan politics.

Polk's boyhood was marked by several distinctive influences. There was an upsetting religious conflict between his parents. There was the upheaval of the family's move from an established community to an unknown frontier destination. There was a continuing, debilitating pattern of poor health. There was a privileged and focused education. But perhaps most influential was his intense political indoctrination at the family hearth. "He grew up imbued with the principles of . . . Jefferson," wrote George Bancroft, the historian who served in his cabinet.[2]

His maturation as a Jeffersonian Republican and then as a Jacksonian Democrat is the aspect of his life easiest to track. Eugene McCormac, his biographer, simply concluded that Polk's faith in Republican doctrine was "inherited."[3] It is quite clear that from early childhood both his grandfather and his father engraved on the boy's mind a political creed that never faded. For Ezekiel and Sam Polk, Republican philosophy was their gospel; Jefferson was their Jesus. Born on Little Sugar Creek near Charlotte, North Carolina, in 1795—just four years after the nation had ratified the Bill of Rights—Polk was three years old when President John Adams signed the Sedition Act, which sought to kill public censure of his Federalist policies. Jim Polk was six by the time Jefferson, having defeated Adams in 1800, pardoned those Republican critics who had been convicted of castigating Federalists under the act.

While the boy was much too young to understand everything he heard around the family table in Mecklenburg County, the demonizing of John Adams, Alexander Hamilton, and Federalist principles seemed to comport with what he knew of the world. Jefferson was the first president he remembered, his first political hero, the leader his elders believed in and admired. In simplest terms, there was an ongoing contest between Jefferson's adherents and his enemies, the power elite.

As Polk grew into adulthood, everything he had grasped about the conflict between Federalist and Republican values seemed to reinforce a basic and logical argument that the country would be better served if national government was the declared servant of all the people (or all those who were not slaves) and was barred from acting chiefly as the agent of rich and powerful constituencies.

Jackson was the heir to the Jeffersonian philosophy, as Henry Clay was to the creed of Hamilton. Polk knew where he was in that fight, and it became his own.

GOD AND FAMILY

But if there was agreement in the household as it related to politics, there was discord when it came to Polk's early religious life. As a newborn babe, he was thrust into the eye of a spiritual storm. In his Mecklenburg community, where Presbyterianism was as common as patriotism, he was a marked child: unbaptized.*

Following their marriage, his parents, Samuel and Jane Knox Polk, attended the Presbyterian congregation at Providence, a farming community a few miles from where they lived along Sugar Creek. Polk's mother was a great-grandniece of John Knox, the religionist who brought the Reformation to Scotland, and was delighted when Sam agreed that their son, born just ten months and seven days after their Christmas Day marriage in 1794, would be given her family name and baptized in her family's tradition.

The moment came when the Reverend James Wallis, a stern and dogmatic pastor, expected the child's parents to affirm their Christian faith. Sam balked. He would make no such avowal. Whereupon Pastor Wallis also balked; no parental commitment to the Christian faith, no baptism, he decreed. It was not until fifty-three years later, on his deathbed, that James K. Polk was christened by a Methodist minister.

The controversy in which the pastor visited the sin of the father on the son had its roots in a two-year-old argument between Reverend Wallis and Sam's opinionated, confrontational, deist father. Ezekiel fell out with the minister in April 1793 after his second wife bore him a stillborn son, who, according to the pastor's doctrinal

*Among Polk's biographers, Charles Sellers provides the most detailed account of this family religious controversy.

belief, would be denied admittance to heaven. Grandfather Polk declared unholy war against Reverend Wallis, seeking, without great success, to convert the preacher's church members to deism. Into that abrasive religious environment, Polk was born.

Jim's childhood and formal education were interlaced with religious orientation and tension. Certainly his mother's piety was a positive force. His father's absorbing values were materialistic, with a near-religious dedication to commerce, farming, and building wealth.

Soon after his marriage Polk dutifully paid for a pew in the Presbyterian Church, and throughout his life he often found time to attend Sunday services with his wife, Sarah. As a young, ambitious politician, he became a Mason and signed on with the state militia, but never joined a religious congregation.

During Polk's years of public service, as throughout most of the nation's life, religion mattered in society. Alexis de Tocqueville, who arrived from France in 1831 (when Congressman Polk was thirty-six), wrote, "The religious aspect of the country was the first thing that struck my attention." He was "astonished" by the "peaceful dominion" of religious tolerance throughout the United States. He was told by clergymen and laity alike that it was due "mainly to the separation of church and state." Tocqueville never met Pastor Wallis but did discover "men full of a fanatical and almost wild spiritualism" across the country. He concluded that "religious insanity is very common in the United States."[4] Separation of church and state, in those days, as now, did not keep preachers out of politics. (Jefferson was attacked during the 1800 presidential campaign by a Connecticut minister for being a "howling atheist.") Nor did the "wall of separation" deter politicians from openly seeking denominational support. (In his first race for Congress Madison pledged to support a Bill of Rights in order to win Baptist backing.)

In his presidential diary, Polk occasionally mentions the quality of a sermon he heard at church with Sarah, but more as if he were a theater critic than a worshipper. The churchgoing was at Sarah's initiative. Most often he notes in his diary that he "accompanied his wife" to church. She had no hesitation in interrupting a Sunday-morning presidential conference by walking into his office and inviting (it may have been a demand) the assembled conferees to attend with her.

Rarely in his life did he speak on his religious commitment. When expressing a slight partiality for the Methodist Church, he comes across more as if he were considering which fork in a road to take for a comfortable horseback ride, rather than selecting a path to salvation.

As president, he rarely referred to God in his diary or suggested that he prayed for guidance or heavenly intervention in his life— not even during the war with Mexico. On one occasion, after an angry argument with a preacher, he did "thank God" for the constitutional wall between government and religion.[5] Once, when frustrated by individuals seeking official appointments, he promised that if "a kind Providence [permitted him] length of days and health," he would write "the secret and hitherto unknown history" of the evil workings of government.[6] Again, the deity turned up in the diary when he discussed with his cabinet how to handle the growing difficulties with Great Britain and Mexico. The country should stand firm against both countries, said Polk, "and leave the rest to God and the country."[7] But religion was second to politics in Polk's life.

In his inaugural address, he followed the example of every one of his predecessors with a paragraph invoking "the aid of that Almighty Ruler of the Universe . . . to guard this Heaven-favored land."[8] On his fiftieth birthday, in office not yet a year, after a church service, he wrote that the scriptural text that day had set him thinking: "Before fifty years more would expire I would be sleeping with the generations which have gone before me. I thought of the vanity of this world's honors and . . . that it was

time for me to be 'putting my house in order.'"[9] He didn't mention it again for three years. On his fifty-third birthday he
returned to the theme, repeating almost as a premonition: "I will
soon go the way of all earth. I pray God to prepare me to meet the
great event."[10] Seven months later he was dead.

However he treated religion in his own life, he had a clear
understanding of where it belonged in the life of the nation. In
1846, in the midst of the expansionist movement and the north-
westward sweep toward the Oregon Territory, he encouraged the
measured movement of persecuted Mormons (whose members
had voted for him) as part of the migration. There was strong
political opposition to it. When Senator James Semple came to
see him to criticize "absurd" Mormon religious practices and to
urge that Polk halt their move, he flatly refused. "If I could interfere with the Mormons, I could with the Baptists or any other religious sect," he said.[11]

Brigham Young had written an impassioned letter to Polk in
May 1845, asking the government's protection from the brutal
persecution Mormons had suffered in Missouri and in Semple's
Illinois. A year later, when Jesse C. Little, a Mormon from New
Hampshire, came to investigate the administration's attitude
toward the Mormons' planned move to Oregon, the president
assured him that he believed the Mormons were entitled to the
same constitutional protection as every other denomination. He
then asked Little's help in recruiting as many as five hundred Mormon men to join the army to fight against Mexico. Again, it was
politics first!

Earlier the president had expressed grave concerns that the
Roman Catholic population of Mexico feared that if their country
were conquered by the United States, Polk's army would close
and rob their churches. He asked Bishop John Hughes of the
Catholic Diocese of New York to send to Mexico a number of
Spanish-speaking American priests to convince the Mexican

clergy and laity that the United States would never interfere with their religion.

Polk found Hughes "highly intelligent and agreeable"[12] when he pledged to help—and even volunteered to travel personally to Mexico—to communicate Polk's assurances to the Mexican archbishop. Five months later there was a backlash from a Protestant preacher. Polk's hot castigations of his political enemies singe the pages of his diary, but he saved his most searing outburst for the Reverend William L. McCalla, a Presbyterian who brought a petition that Polk called "a violent and most intolerant attack on the Roman Catholics and a censure on the administration."[13] "Aside from its abuse of Catholics and its fanaticism," said Polk, the memo's main point "was that unless I appointed the Rev. McCalla a chaplain, the petitioners intended to go before the public and attack the administration upon religious grounds because of the employment of these Catholic priests. I felt great contempt for Mr. McCalla and his religion and gave him my mind freely."[14]

"Thank God," Polk told McCalla, that "under our Constitution there was no connection between church and state and . . . as President of the United States I recognized no distinction of creeds in my appointments to office." He explained to the minister that he had asked the Catholic clergy to help change the mindset of what he called the "ignorant people" of Mexico. McCalla was "a knave without vital religion or a fanatic without reason . . . destitute of both religion and principle."[15] It is interesting to ponder how the unbaptized president might have fared as a candidate a century and a half later in a political environment infused with fundamentalist theology akin to the righteousness of Pastor Wallis.

Polk may have been ultimately touched by his mother's fervor, or he may have been true to the anticlerical, deist leanings of Ezekiel and Sam. He died a nonpracticing Methodist who ardently believed in Jefferson's wall of separation between church and state.

THE POLKS OF NORTH CAROLINA

They were liberty-loving folk, the Polks of Mecklenburg. No doubt young Jim heard the story of how his great-uncle Thomas Polk reacted after word reached North Carolina that British troops had fired on American citizens at Lexington and Concord. Tom Polk was a firebrand, who stepped forward to speak for the crowd of angry North Carolinians that met at Mecklenburg on May 31, 1775, to strip themselves of all ties with King George. "All commissions, civil or military, granted by the Crown . . . are hereby null and void," declared Tom as he read the Mecklenburg Resolves.[16] It was part of the family lore, and probably true, that grandfather Ezekiel was at his older brother Tom's side that day.

As the Polks loved liberty, they also coveted land. Tom Polk was politically wired to North Carolina's foremost power broker of the day: William Blount, architect of the infamous 1783 Land Grab Act, which triggered the surge of exploration, speculation, and exploitation of the western lands. Most Americans looked at that acreage between the Smoky Mountains and the Mississippi River—the Tennessee Territory—as a dangerous no-man's-land of savage Indians, raging streams, and wild animals. Blount, Tom Polk, and their syndicate envisioned an elongated corridor of fertile terrain that would become a strip of towns and cities, plantations and farms settled, developed, and cultivated by a wave of new frontiersmen. Using their political muscle and contacts, the Blount syndicate purchased cheap land warrants from North Carolina's Revolutionary War veterans and ultimately came to control perhaps three million acres of the Tennessee Territory.

Young Jim Polk was also steeped in family stories about Grandfather Ezekiel's frequent explorations to "the West." As Ezekiel traveled, surveyed, claimed, and staked out land developments, his sponsors in the Blount syndicate became more affluent—and he shared a piece of their wealth. Jim was eight years old when his grandfather left North Carolina the last time, bound for Tennessee. Sam kept his family in Mecklenburg for a time. He and Jane were worried about the episodic illnesses that plagued Jim, and Jane's religious life was more tranquil with her father-in-law gone.

Three years later, family reports of the garden spot Ezekiel had found near Columbia in middle Tennessee finally convinced Sam that the fields were much greener and the harvest more rewarding on the other side of the Smokies. With Jim now eleven, he convinced Jane that they should make the move. It was an arduous odyssey that must have been difficult for the ailing boy, who was old enough for some responsibility but not strong enough to assume it. In little more than six weeks the family traversed five hundred miles over paths and roads that were rutted and difficult. It was beyond Polk's comprehension, of course, that one day he would lead the nation west to the Pacific Ocean.

THE YOUTH BECOMES THE MAN

Without a smile at the oxymoron, Polk wrote in his presidential diary that in his youth he had "enjoyed bad health."[17] In childhood he was slightly built, emaciated, and without much strength or energy. Recurring bouts of stomach disorders sapped his vigor and made strenuous work or even play difficult. As George Bancroft said, his "boyhood was . . . very serious and sober."[18] Later, during one of his gubernatorial campaigns, he recalled that as a boy he had cut cane along Tennessee's Duck River, and his early biographers recorded that he had accompanied his father on surveying trips, tending the horses and preparing meals. He no doubt did what he could, but the near-chronic sickness often left him physically unable to carry his load of chores. His ailments naturally frightened and puzzled his parents.[19]

Polk men lived by a strong work ethic. Sam, at one point, decided that perhaps a mercantile career might be less strenuous than farming and arranged for Jim to work for a friend in a

Columbia general store. It didn't take. What Jim craved was formal schooling.

His education, however, was substantially delayed "in consequence of having been very much afflicted."[20] At age seventeen, his illness was diagnosed as urinary stones (as Bancroft accurately reported), and he underwent major surgery—a lithotomy, or stone removal. While the story of Polk's ailment is not as dramatic as Franklin Roosevelt's polio or Woodrow Wilson's stroke during his term of office, it nonetheless is gripping.

For one thing, medical science in the early nineteenth century had not developed a general anesthesia, and the pain inflicted on Jim during the operation was excruciating. For another, since there was no antisepsis to prevent infection, it was dangerous. Several Polk biographers misidentified the surgery as an operation for "gallstones"—a cholecystectomy, in medical jargon—and thereby failed to expose perhaps the most intimate secret of the future president's private life. The operation for urinary stones is the compelling and obvious explanation for his childless marriage; it rendered him sterile or impotent.*

Once Sam understood that his son needed an operation, he sought out the best surgeon available. There is some question as to who that physician of choice was. The best evidence is to be found in Polk's 1844 authorized presidential campaign biography—a common practice of the day—written by J. George Harris and published in ten articles in the *Nashville Union*, Polk's Tennessee political voice.[21]

---

*I am indebted to several medical professionals for their advice on this point. All agree that, while retrospective diagnosis is risky, the surgical procedure (1) could not have been for gallstones and (2) could well have resulted in sterility, impotency, or both. I am particularly indebted to Dr. Dean Knoll, a noted urologist, for his detailed exposition of the implications of the surgery and to Dr. Robert Ikard, whose article in the *Tennessee Historical Quarterly* (summer 1984) first raised this possibility. Others on whom I relied for their thoughtful expertise were Dr. Bernard Brody, Dr. Frank Boehm, Dr. William Ewers, and Dr. John Sergent.

Harris reported that Dr. Philip Syng Physick, of Philadelphia, known as the "American Father of Surgery," was the physician Sam selected. According to this account, the boy was placed in a bed in a covered wagon and, accompanied by an unnamed uncle, set out overland on the eight-hundred-mile trip to Physick's hospital.

En route, Jim suffered continued attacks, and, as the travelers neared Lexington, Kentucky, "he was seized by a paroxysm more painful than any that had preceded it."[22] A change in plans was called for, and the horse-drawn ambulance headed to Danville, where Dr. Ephraim McDowell, another noted medical pioneer, resided and practiced.[23] By modern standards, the operation was a "terrifying procedure." It occurred "under whatever sedation [was] obtainable from brandy." Jim's legs were "held high in the air, and being restrained by straps and assistants, the operation was done as quickly as possible. The procedure was to cut into the perineum (the area immediately behind the scrotum and in front of the anus) with a knife and thence through the prostate into the bladder with a gorget, a pointed, sharp instrument designed for this purpose."[24] The stones then were removed with forceps or a scoop.

As able as McDowell was and as quick as he had to be, the procedure must have meant a hellish half hour of sheer torture for Jim Polk, and a recovery period of weeks before he could return home. Considering the crude methodology involved, the probable tearing of ejaculatory ducts, tissue, nerves, and arteries as the gorget penetrated the prostate, there can be little doubt that the operation left him unable to father a child.

Yet in another sense, the boy became a man on Dr. McDowell's operating table. Here, for the first time, were evidences of the courage, grit, and unyielding iron will that Whigs, the British Crown, and the Mexican army would encounter once he became president.

The operation a success, Sam and Jane agreed to provide Jim with what he wanted most: a formal education. As soon as his surgical scars healed, they sent him off to a Presbyterian academy in the Mount Zion community near Columbia, whose headmaster was the Reverend Robert Henderson. The oldest boy in his class, with no previous exposure to Latin or Greek, he nonetheless excelled and won the praise of headmaster Henderson for "exemplary" moral conduct.[25] His parents next dispatched him to Murfreesboro, a thriving small town closer to Nashville, where the more advanced Bradley Academy was located. There the Reverend Samuel Black, another Presbyterian, presided over a curriculum that included literature and logic, philosophy and geography, and more Latin and Greek. Again, Jim did well and was judged "the most promising young man in the school."[26]

Over the family's decade of residence in Tennessee, Sam had expanded his commercial interests and was among the community's most creative and successful business entrepreneurs—a land surveyor like his father; the land agent for vast properties owned in Tennessee by the University of North Carolina; and a substantial landowner in his own right. In time Sam captured regional mail delivery contracts, opened a general store, was partner in a steamboat enterprise, and became a guiding director of Columbia's first bank.

Impressed by his son's obvious passion for learning, Sam decided to send him to the University of North Carolina at Chapel Hill, where he breezed through the entrance examination and was admitted as a sophomore in 1816. The president of the university, the Reverend Robert Chapman, was another Presbyterian. Bible study was at the base of all other instruction at the university, moral philosophy serving as the foundation upon which the school determined that an informed young man would build a career. Whatever dissident religious views Jim had picked up listening to his father and grandfather, he carefully kept to himself.

Shortly after he began attending classes, a student revolt erupted over an administration censorship issue. Jim remained on the periphery, poring over such subjects as Cicero, Homer, quadratic equations, and conic sections, while a near-riot briefly closed down the school in September 1816.

It was the Dialectic Society, one of the school's competing debate clubs, that gave early expression to the life Polk would pursue in law and government. In one of his speeches, he expressed concerns that some of the nation's leaders were flirting with foreign, monarchical ideas, polluting the pure stream of American republicanism and undermining individual liberties. He nailed Alexander Hamilton, the Federalist foe of Jefferson, as "a friend to aristocracy," a would-be royalist voice of a dangerous power elite.[27]

The university was loaded with young men whose minds were bent toward politics and public service. William Haywood would become a senator from North Carolina. John Y. Mason would be in Polk's cabinet. William B. Shepard and George Dromgoogle, both active in the student revolt, served in Congress, and William D. Moseley, Polk's roommate, became governor of Florida. There were several future state legislators and even an Episcopal bishop. Polk's scholastic achievements outstripped those of all the other students. At graduation he had earned the right to deliver the commencement address.

Historians have criticized Polk's lack of creativity, his gray imagination, his intellectual rigidity, his inability to think outside the box. Yet he had a keen, logical, absorbent mind. His formal education provided him with the capacity to digest facts and apply them to academic problems—and, later in life, to legal and political ones. He strove to become eloquent, and he exhorted his classmates in one of his declamations to develop "that fluency of language, that connexion of ideas and boldness of delivery" that would serve them "in the council, in the pulpit and at the bar."[28]

CLERK AND LAWYER

To gain admission to the bar in those days, it was necessary to be accepted into a certified law firm to study cases and precedents under the guidance of a licensed practitioner. Polk had the great luck to be accepted in the chambers of Felix Grundy, the giant of the state's criminal bar, who had moved to Tennessee from Kentucky, where he had served both as a state legislator and as chief justice of the state supreme court. He had the eloquence Polk sought for himself. His talent for anaphora was legendary. An admirer wrote that under Grundy's oratorical spell "great assemblies . . . tremble and shudder . . . enlightened galleries have wept and fainted."[29] Polk and Grundy became close friends and political allies, serving together in the Tennessee legislature (where often they were on opposite sides of issues), in the Tennessee congressional delegation (where most often they were on the same side), and in Jackson's presidential campaigns.

For more than a year Polk studied at Grundy's Nashville office, and with his mentor's help landed a job as clerk for the state senate. It was the perfect move at precisely the right moment. From the day the youthful clerk walked into the senate chamber in the Rutherford County courthouse, he knew he was right where he wanted to be: close to the action, working, albeit in a subordinate's role, with power brokers and deal cutters, observing up close their conduct as they walked the line between legislative principle and political compromise.

For him, there was none of the proverbial smell of sausage-making in creating law. He was enamored with the process. Shortly after the state legislature adjourned in the spring of 1820, Grundy found Polk ready to be tested by the Tennessee Supreme Court. He passed the court's bar examination in June and was admitted officially to the practice of law.

It was not the best of times for a young man to be entering business. The entire nation had suffered near-economic collapse in the Panic of 1819, and Tennessee was not spared the pain. By mid-1820 cotton prices were plummeting, banks were making harsh demands on borrowers, and the lending institutions were being pressured to deal in hard money—gold and silver—to back up paper notes they had issued.

The financial problems of ordinary people, however, some-times enhance the fortunes of lawyers. In the months after the depression set in, there were five hundred lawsuits filed in middle Tennessee for the collection of debts. Polk's practice prospered.

Sam Polk's pockets also were deep enough to get by the difficult times. He welcomed the young lawyer home to Columbia with a log cabin office and a modest library of law books. Through all his years in Congress, Polk continued to practice law when not in Washington. Seven lawyers who became presidents are known to have taken cases all the way to the U.S. Supreme Court, and Polk is one of them. In January 1827 the Court agreed with the argument of Polk and his co-counsel in the case *Williams v. Norris*.

Polk's days in the Dialectic Society at Chapel Hill prepared him well for the law. As a courtroom advocate, he was, according to his biographer John Jenkins, "wary and skillful, but frank and honorable [and] in addressing a jury he was always animated and impressive in manner."[30] The ultimate compliment came from his mentor Grundy, in a trial that pitted the two friends against each other. At one point the older lawyer told the judge, "I believe, may't please the court, that I have been preparing a club here with which my own head is to be broken."[31]

Polk's early practice included land disputes, note collection, and debt and billing claims. He got payment for a client named John S. Williamson, who asked him to negotiate with his debtors for cash, "whiskey money," and slaves. On one occasion Polk collected $1,000 for him and sent it by courier, deducting $10 as his 1 percent fee. When the "whiskey money" was in hand, Polk "cut the notes in two" and sent the halves by separate mail, to protect his client from robbery.[32] His cousin William Polk's correspondence from North Carolina included plainspoken instructions: collect a debt and interest; bring suit immediately; send the money "as fast as the law will admit."[33] The young lawyer deposited $1,072.10 in the Columbia bank to William's credit. By now his fee was up to 2½ percent. Such was the practice of Tennessee law in 1820.

By March 1822, clerking in the state senate had infected Polk with candidate fever. In a letter to a former school chum he noted that "Old Yancey"—William Yancey, a two-term legislator—would seek reelection.[34] As he wrote, Polk was himself traveling the backwoods homesites of Maury County, testing the temperature of the political waters. By September he had decided to wade into the stream. "I am a candidate for the H. Rept. in the Tennessee Legislature and I am opposed by the former representative Yancey," he wrote William Polk.[35] Incumbent Yancey would become a "former" legislator when Polk defeated him in 1823.

There was no secret ballot in those days. Voters simply walked into the precinct place, paid their poll tax, and declared for a candidate. It may have been Polk's energy and attractiveness, the standing of Sam and Jane Polk in the community, or the whiskey he provided at the polling places, but when the vote was announced he had won handily.

He was a young man on the move and on the make. In 1820 he joined the Masons. In 1821 he signed up with the local militia, commissioned with the rank of captain, then elevated to colonel. He did little to earn the rank. A title, however, was a political necessity. Later Jackson usually referred to him in letters as "Colonel Polk."

And then there was romance. Women were attracted to James K. Polk. There was in Columbia a young woman named Catherine, a "plenitude of perfection," who, his friend Jesse Egnew wrote, spoke his name with "wonted sweetness."[36] He was a good-looking young man, short and still slender, dark-haired, square-jawed with a countenance almost too serious to believe. However many Catherines there might have been, there was only one comely Sarah Childress—and she was in Murfreesboro. By 1822, that is where his heart was. Her older brother Anderson had been his classmate at Bradley Academy back in 1814. Certainly they had met in passing, but he was then nineteen, Sarah only eleven.

She, on the other hand, must have been impressed with her brother's schoolmate—older than any other student and the academic leader at Bradley. What a difference a few years can make—and did. Her father, Joel Childress, a prosperous farmer and tavern owner, died while she was still in finishing school in North Carolina. Sarah remained home with her grieving mother, and there she again saw Polk, who was clerking in the senate.

By early 1822, the well-dressed, well-spoken, twenty-six-year-old candidate-lawyer–militia captain was seriously pursuing her. Sometime early the following year he proposed, and, to the delight of her widowed mother, they were married New Year's Day, 1824, just five months after his victory over Old Yancey. Sam's wedding presents included Elias, a slave boy who would remain with them, as an indentured servant, throughout Polk's life.

Sarah's personality—outgoing, vivacious, and witty—was a natural complement to her husband's formal reserve. She brought out the best in him, even prompting him to joke after their wedding (and he rarely joked) that had he remained a lowly clerk in the senate, she never would have married him. Sarah apprehended that she had married a public man, and that it would be necessary for her to become a public woman. She came to the role naturally.

In his first year in Congress, alone in a Washington boardinghouse with other representatives of the federal government, he longed for Sarah to be with him. And her letters reflect that she did not want him to be without her. There is no way to know whether Polk suffered from anaphrodisia, but she could show flashes of jealousy. When he was away campaigning at the height of the 1843 race for governor, she wrote tartly, "[I am] pleased to find that you had time to play the beaux in receiving flowers from young ladies for I am sure you did not act the beaux toward your wife when at home."[37]

2

Old and Young Hickory

Polk's career was grafted as a limb to the trunk of Jackson's political tree, which gave it sustenance. As a young man, Jackson acted as if the laws of political gravity did not apply to him. Even as he served as Tennessee's first congressman, one of its early U.S. senators, and a member of the highest court in the state, his exaggerated sense of moral outrage, his burning ambition, and his violent temper led to repeated embarrassing conflicts: dueling, street fighting, gambling disputes, verbal attacks on critics, and explosive tantrums. Thomas Jefferson, looking back on his days as vice president, remembered Senator Jackson as "a dangerous man."[1] When President Monroe was thinking of appointing Jackson minister to Russia, Jefferson warned, "Why Good God! He would breed you a quarrel before he had been there a month."[2]

Jackson was involved in three duels, suffering a bullet wound himself when he killed Charles Dickinson, a Nashvillian with whom he had argued. While still a judge, he twice fought publicly on a Knoxville street and roadside with former governor John Sevier. He was wounded again in a knife and gun battle with Jesse and Thomas Hart Benton. And then there was *the* scandal: he had stolen another man's wife. In his own mind, Jackson held the high moral ground in every conflict, large and small. While there was a charismatic flair about him, it is fair to say that until he became a military messiah he was more respected than admired, more feared than loved.

Jackson went to war with the hostile Creeks, the Seminoles, and the Cherokees, taming, bullying, bribing them out of their land and forcing them into new treaties. Elevated by President Madison from state militia commander to general in the U.S. Army, he crushed the twelve thousand British troops at the Battle of New Orleans, then went on to muscle the Spanish out of Florida. He had made the country safe from foreign and domestic danger, and it had a canonizing effect. By 1821, when President Monroe asked him to become governor of Florida, he was the military patron saint of the land. His brawls, duels, tantrums, threats, and marriage to Rachel Donelson Robards all melded into the Homeric image of a man of honor. What might have been shameful to many now became blameless to almost all but the clique of enemies he had made along the way in Tennessee.

As war broke out with Great Britain in 1812, Polk, just seventeen, was recovering from his operation and thinking of school, not studying war. He had grown up with glimpses of "the General," a friend of both his father and his grandfather. Polk thrilled with the entire nation as news came from New Orleans that American forces lost only seven soldiers, while British casualties totaled two thousand.

Once Jackson's military career was in the ascendancy, he began to think of the presidency. He left political infighting with his enemies at home to the capable hands of two close friends, the lawyer, judge, and banker John Overton and former governor Willie Blount. Their organization guided his presidential campaigns.

From the day Tennessee became a state until Jackson was elected president, Jeffersonian republicanism dominated politics in Tennessee and through the South. The opposition to Jackson came from a small but growing faction of enemies led by Andrew Erwin, a middle Tennessee legislator, planter, and businessman.

Tough and ambitious, Erwin knew that Jackson, as war hero, was unassailable. But he saw Polk, as early as his first race for Congress, as Jackson's natural successor and made the young man his political target. From the outset it was assumed by the anti-Jackson crowd that Polk was Jackson's Maury County protégé, joined, hip and mind, to Jackson. Indeed he was. But though he followed Old Hickory, Polk also studied his hero closely—and noted his mistakes as well as his achievements.

FISCAL POLITICS

To Polk, all politics was fiscal, deeply rooted in the early struggle between federalism and republicanism; Hamilton and Jefferson; the wealthy elite and the common man. He rejected Alexander Hamilton's early conviction that the "rich and wellborn" were entitled to "a distinct and permanent share of the government" while "the mass of the people . . . are turbulent and changing [and] seldom judge or determine right."[3] He rejected Daniel Webster's theory that it was "political wisdom to found government on property" and Noah Webster's belief that "the man who has half a million dollars . . . has a much higher interest in government than the man who has little or no property."[4] Polk believed that if democracy was to have meaning, the great mass of people were as entitled as the wealthy few to vote and to serve in high offices. Beyond that, government had a role to play in providing economic justice for every working citizen—except, of course, women and slaves.

Polk's entry into public life as clerk of the state senate coincided with the Panic of 1819 and gave him his first practical lesson in politics and the economy. The depression hit that year with whirlwind suddenness and created widespread economic devastation. Tennessee suffered, as banks in the state, as across the nation, refused to redeem paper notes with gold and silver, called specie. The boom economy, fed by easy credit, abruptly ended.

Many Tennesseans, up and down the economic ladder, found themselves deeply in debt, holding virtually worthless paper. One businessman forced into bankruptcy was William Carroll, the owner of a Nashville hardware store and nail factory, who had served in 1814–15 as second in command under Jackson at New Orleans. Broke, but popular and persuasive, "Billy" Carroll turned from business to politics, where he would play a key role in Polk's early career.

In 1821, Carroll ran for governor as the avowed candidate of the debtor class. It was a time when all Tennessee political action played out between Republican factions. John Overton, still a prominent banker and power broker, threw support of the Overton-Blount faction to Carroll's opponent, Edward Ward, an old Jackson friend. Andrew Erwin and the anti-Jackson faction went for Carroll, who won a stunning victory with 31,290 votes to 7,294 for Ward.

For the first time the chokehold the Overton-Blount faction had held for decades on Tennessee politics had been weakened. Jackson, who would benefit for years from the support of the Blount-Overton crowd, was serving as governor of Florida during the election, so his popularity was undiminished by Ward's loss.

For Polk, already feeling the pull of politics, the election was his first glimpse of a political conflict between entrenched, moneyed power and an aroused electorate. As senate clerk, he now saw firsthand how Governor Carroll responded to the financial crisis. Carroll's first message to the legislature warned of "the evil consequences" of having too much paper money in circulation: "The moment you issue more [paper money] than is necessary it depreciates," wrote Carroll, "and . . . the price of every commodity in market is increased." Upon what principle of honesty, he asked, could banks violate their contracts to pay off notes with gold and silver?[5]

Polk observed with fascination the battle for the minds and hearts—and perhaps the pocketbooks—of lawmakers as the Carroll administration pushed to force banks to resume redeeming paper with specie. It was obvious to Polk that Jackson's friends represented the private interests, while Carroll was on the side of the people. The clerk knew where he belonged in that fight.

Two years later, in September 1823, with Yancey defeated, Polk arrived as a voting member in the lower legislative body, with banks under pressure to resume payments in gold and silver. There was every reason for the moneyed interests to expect that Polk would be on their side. He was, after all, the son of Sam Polk, a man of business.

Early on, however, Polk sent them a message: They could not count on him. He quickly established himself as Carroll's voice on the house floor. It took enormous self-confidence for Polk. Not only was he going against the potent banking lobby, but the spokesman for the opposition was none other than his old legal sponsor, Felix Grundy. While Polk did not hesitate to challenge his mentor on the banking issue, he found waging war with lending institutions to be difficult. Grundy persuaded the legislature to delay forcing bank resumption of gold and silver until 1826.

Meanwhile, Jackson, convinced that Washington was corrupt to the core, was serious about running for the White House. He resigned as governor of Florida after three months and was at home at the Hermitage in 1822 when Polk launched his legislative fight against the banking interests. Gradually, the General worked himself into an emotional lather against national banking policy, correctly blaming the tight money policies of the Second Bank of the United States for the depression of 1819.

As president, Jackson would declare war on that bank and its president, Nicholas Biddle, who came to head it in 1823. Old Hickory would look upon Biddle as the evil genie who showered key congressional members with favors, gifts, and loans in return for his charter and support for the federal deposits in his bank. Jackson would rely on Polk to help him wage and win the bank war.

As Polk, the freshman legislator, publicly was urging Tennessee banking reform in the general assembly, Jackson growled privately to his friend William B. Lewis, "The constitution of our state as well as the constitution of the United States prohibits the establishment of Banks in every state." It was quite a declaration, since some of Old Hickory's best friends—John Overton and Hugh Lawson White—had sizable banking investments. Much later, President Jackson told Congressman Polk, "Every one that knows me does know that I have always been opposed to the Bank [of the United States], nay, all banks."[6] Polk and Carroll could have used that sort of open denunciation from the popular hero Jackson during their early struggles with Grundy to get banks to resume specie payments.

TWO VOTES FOR JACKSON

His two-year stint in the state legislature was both an exciting and enervating time for Polk. The phrase "Jackson for President" suddenly exploded in the general assembly, and Polk was proud to cast his vote for the resolution projecting his hero's name onto the national stage. The anti-Jackson faction, headed by Andrew Erwin, had gained an upper hand in state politics by riding the coattails of Billy Carroll to the governor's office in 1821, but Erwin was too smart to oppose the presidential resolution nominating Old Hickory. His crowd, like many of Jackson's friends, thought the legislative nomination would not reverberate much beyond Tennessee's borders. The Overton-Blount faction—pro-Jackson but also pro-banking—had lost favor when Carroll had been elected. They thought talk of Jackson's presidential prospects would rebuild their reputation among the Tennessee electorate. They were using him. Hugh Lawson White, Jackson's friend at the time, thought it all an unfunny joke. He was right.

Andrew Erwin, aware that Jackson had said he would "support the Devil" before he would support Secretary of the Treasury William H. Crawford, was leading the anti-Jacksonians to back Crawford for president.[7] Worried that he would be shut out of power, John Overton, without telling Jackson, began making overtures to Henry Clay, who was to be a candidate. Then, astonishingly, Jackson's candidacy caught fire. He was a national sensation. Jackson seemed not in the least surprised at the phenomenal public reaction to his candidacy. For him, this would be a people's holy cause to rid the government of evil men and dark dealings. Now with a serious candidate on his hands, Overton forgot about Clay.

Overton joined with two other Jackson friends, John Eaton and William B. Lewis, in launching a Jackson crusade. The first order of business was to defeat the incumbent U.S. senator John Williams, who was hostile to Jackson's candidacy. There was a problem. Williams was popular with the state legislators, who at that time elected the senators. Overton, Eaton, and Lewis could find no candidate strong enough to unseat him—except Old Hickory himself. Jackson had no desire to go back to the U.S. Senate. He had hated his earlier tenure there. However, his presidential campaign could not tolerate a Tennessee senator in Washington working against him. He came to the state capital from the Hermitage to ask legislators for their support and was elected senator by a vote of 35 to 25—hardly a landslide, but a comfortable victory. One of those thirty-five votes came from James K. Polk. He always would say with pride that he voted "Jackson" twice during his two years in the general assembly.

THE CONGRESSIONAL CANDIDATE

As the presidential election excitement was nearing its peak in August 1824, Polk announced his candidacy for Congress. No one could have been more elated than Polk when Jackson's tide of popular votes inundated John Quincy Adams, Crawford, and Clay; and no member of the Jackson campaign team could have felt the pain of the Adams-Clay deal—the "corrupt bargain" that effected Jackson's defeat—more than he. Another idealistic young man might have been turned off by the smell of it. Not Polk. That "bargain" was his incentive to get into politics more deeply. This was a wrong to be righted. The place for him was in Congress. There was a flood of sympathetic support for Jackson everywhere as word of the "corrupt bargain" spread. When Old Hickory endorsed Polk among a five-candidate field, his election was assured.

From the distance of a century and three quarters, Andrew Erwin's decision to challenge Polk for Congress that year almost seems suicidal. Perhaps he thought the other three candidates, all Jackson supporters, would peel ballots off Polk's vote totals. Perhaps he expected support from Carroll since his machine had backed Billy for governor. But Polk had been Carroll's voice on the legislative floor against the banking lobby. He was awarded a colonel's commission on the governor's staff. And Billy Carroll was too wise to alienate Jackson.

Erwin focused his criticism of Polk on a single issue: "internal improvements." While today federal funding of transportation and its infrastructure includes money for interstate highways, airports, railways, dams, bridges, and waterways, there was a time when many politicians considered it against the public interest for the national government to support such projects. That was the Republican position, grounded in Jefferson's fear, embraced later by Jacksonian Democrats, that if a president had the authority to grant "internal improvements," it would dangerously empower his administration to reward friends and punish enemies. Republicans held that each state should decide what projects it needed and could afford. As John Jenkins pointed out, "The subject of internal improvements was the only political question of importance" in Polk's congressional race—except for the corrupt bargain.[8]

Already Polk had voted in the general assembly against a Nashville-to-Columbia toll road because it required a state commitment to a private entrepreneur who would build and operate the toll road at a profit. That vote, said Erwin, gave voters an idea that Polk's true sentiments were hostile to public works projects to benefit the people. There was a larger issue in the works. A gigantic federal project, the proposed Buffalo-to–New Orleans roadway, was pending in Congress. It was designed to tie cities, far north and south, to Washington. Erwin promised he would push to get a leg of it for middle Tennessee. Polk, he suggested, would be delighted to let it go to North Carolina.

Unfortunately for Erwin, the marriage of his son to Henry Clay's daughter had put a familial taint from the "corrupt bargain" on his campaign, and he now sought to turn the Clay negative into an advantage. Elect him, he told the voters, and he would use his in-law's influence with Clay, "the champion of internal improve-ments,"[9] to get the national roadway through Tennessee. That argu-ment had resonance. Clay's grand scheme for the nation's future growth was all wrapped up in something he called the American System, which included massive internal improvements. He would have pled guilty to the charge that these public works projects would win popular support for the Adams presidency.

Erwin's jibes had more than a needling effect on Polk. Under growing pressure to give the electorate a formal answer on inter-nal improvements, he drafted a statement that reflects the first trace of cynicism in his politics. There was, he said, "a question of some difficulty" in determining "how far the general government has power to make internal improvements." Yes, the improve-ments often contributed to the nation's "wealth, prosperity, and convenience." They improved mail delivery and aided movement of troops in wartime. But how far could the federal government go before crossing a line that infringed on the power and rights of states? He waffled. He favored, he said, "a judicious system of Internal Improvements."[10] He left it to his supporters to argue that the Buffalo-to–New Orleans road project was "judicious."

He knew he was flirting with Republican heresy, but he wor-ried that the issue might cost him the election. His strategy worked. On Election Day, 90 percent of white men in the district turned out and gave him a clear margin of victory: 3,669 votes for Polk to 2,748 for Erwin.

Still, the issue of internal improvements was like a barge floating in midstream of a building current. Slowly, inexorably, it was moving toward a port of public acceptance. Once elected, Polk reconverted to strict Republican ideology on the issue. In Congress, as a member and later as Speaker, he consistently held the line opposed to these federal projects. As president, he twice vetoed internal improvements bills.

THE WILL OF THE PEOPLE

Polk turned thirty a month and three days before he was sworn in as a member of the U.S. House of Representatives. The politics of the city of Washington had changed significantly in the quarter century since 1800, when it had succeeded Philadelphia as the seat of government. Thomas Jefferson's election that year over John Adams sent the Federalist party into a decline from which it would never recover. Republicanism (the official party designation in 1801 became Democratic-Republican) was the only viable political party when Polk came to the nation's capital. John Quincy Adams was elected under the party banner.

For Congressman Polk, however, the spirit of federalism survived dangerously in the mind of John Quincy Adams, son of the last Federalist president, and in the mind of his secretary of state, Henry Clay.

At the start, Polk had one compelling issue on his mind: to right the wrong done to Andrew Jackson by amending the Constitution and taking away the power of the House of Representatives to defeat the will of the voters in future presidential elections. A newcomer in strange surroundings, he mingled with colleagues but remained silent during his first few weeks. George McDuffie of South Carolina and D. P. Cook of Illinois introduced resolutions to alter the Twelfth Amendment, which dealt with presidential elections, a direct slap in the face of Adams and Clay and many sitting members of Congress who had put the president in the White House. Despite strong public opinion favoring the McDuffie and Cook proposals, this was to be a hard-fought and losing battle. The debate, hot and extended, was still raging on March 23, when Polk rose to make his maiden speech before the House.

The Adams-Clay crowd had argued that government was safer in the hands of informed elected representatives, whose judgment could check the passions of ill-informed citizen-voters. Since childhood, everything Polk had come to believe condemned this Federalist model. Once on his feet, Polk's Democratic impulses took voice. The best possible government, he asserted, was one "based upon the will of the people" and grounded in the ideal that "all power emanates from them." Government by an elite minority was antithetical to a liberty-loving society. "The majority should rule and the minority should submit," he declared.[11] When it came to selecting the president, it was the business of the people, not of Congress. When a matter as important as the presidency was at stake, he said, members of Congress might be subject to the influence of bribes or venal patronage. The reference cut close to the bone of the "bargain." As he said it, Polk looked into the faces of members who had voted to reject the will of the people in favor of the will of Henry Clay.

Edward Everett of Massachusetts sought to change the subject. Members of the House, he said, having taken an oath to uphold the Constitution, were powerless to change it. That, snapped Polk, was a "puerile conception." Corruption was the point he wanted to hammer home. "Shall we assume to ourselves the high prerogative of being uncontaminated and incorruptible. . . . Is immaculate purity to be found within these walls and no other corner of the earth?"[12]

Everett then took a slap at Jackson. The real threat to the nation, he contended, would come from "a president elected by an overwhelming majority; some military chieftain that should arise in the land."

Polk exploded. "Some military chieftain? Yes sir! By some military chieftain whose only crime it was to have served his country faithfully at a period when that country needed . . . his services."[13]

Certainly Polk, McDuffie, and Cook got the best of the argument in the public forum. It was, however, a losing effort. The Clay and Adams forces in the House prevailed.

As the session wore on, Polk voted most often as an obstructionist to administration proposals. Eugene McCormac described much of his opposition as "political claptrap."[14]

It was just such claptrap that his constituents in the Sixth Congressional District wanted to hear. In 1827 the anti-Jackson crowd supported Lunsford Bramlett of Giles County against Polk, but the latter won again handily with 6,350 votes to Bramlett's 4,846. Polk's seat in Congress was secure. He would be elected seven times before he resigned to run for governor in 1839.

As proud as he was over his success in Tennessee, Polk was depressed and soured by the political environment in Washington under Adams and Clay. To his cousin Will Polk in North Carolina he complained bitterly that key committees of both houses of Congress were "arranged for effect," loaded to tilt in favor of the Adams administration. "Such has been . . . the influence of power," he said, complaining that "the great lever of public patronage is corruptly used [by Adams and Clay] . . . to sustain an administration who never came to power by the voice of the people."[15] Later, ironically, Polk would exercise "the influence of power" as ruthlessly and as manipulatively as Adams and Clay ever did.

For Jackson's closest advisers—John Eaton, William B. Lewis, and John Overton—it was clear soon after Adams took over the White House that Old Hickory's presidential run had been deterred but not derailed. The new 1828 campaign was an extension of the losing debacle in 1824. Polk, always eager to help, thought Eaton and Lewis were taking personal advantage of their relationship with Jackson. Polk knew the two old cronies vested little trust in him because of his early stand against banks. He found breaking into the Jackson inner circle difficult.

While his correspondence with Jackson edged him closer to his hero, Polk remained outside the circle. His first real chance at making a meaningful contribution came in early 1826, when Jackson decided to create a Washington newspaper, the *United States Telegraph*. The publication's mission was to attack the Adams administration regularly and to support Jackson's efforts to build an image as heroic victim. John Eaton, heavily involved in running the continuing campaign, asked Polk to provide financial support for the paper, which was to be edited by Duff Green, a close friend and kinsman of Vice President John C. Calhoun. Polk readily agreed. Jackson personally put three thousand dollars into the enterprise.

The newspaper venture was an indication of a growing friendship between Jackson and Calhoun, whose friends also helped finance the publication. In the campaign of 1824, Calhoun had been as ambitious as Adams and Clay, but he felt the mushrooming of support for Jackson and had decided to run as the sole candidate for vice president. He had no wish to be identified with the Adams administration. Clay realized what was now afoot and commented that "the vice president . . . is up to the hub with the opposition."[16]

As Congressman Polk and his wife arrived in Washington after his reelection in 1827, they found themselves living in the same boardinghouse with the vice president. Also present in the residence of Ann Peyton was Hugh Lawson White, who had been elected to Jackson's Senate seat in 1825—and who later, incidentally, would marry the widowed landlady. Others in the house included Polk's Tennessee colleague (and future enemy) John Bell and two senators who were Calhoun allies, Levi Woodbury of New Hampshire and Littleton Tazewell of Virginia. As the boarders met for meals, the ears of Adams and Clay must have been burning. For the moment they were a close-knit group of allies with a common interest in the presidential cause of Andrew Jackson. With the exception of Polk, however, there would come a time when all of those who resided under Ann Peyton's roof would break with Old Hickory.

Henry Clay understood that in order to reelect Adams, Jackson's heroic image had to be tarnished. When the administration's anti-Jackson assault came, it was ugly. Every past indiscretion of Old Hickory's life (and there were enough of them) now was revived and rehashed by the press friendly to Adams and Clay. With the election still a year and a half away, a series of circulars was reproduced in every section of the country branding Jackson a murderer, slave trader, adulterer, cockfighter, gambler, and son of a prostitute who married a mulatto. One of them, the "Coffin Handbill," claimed that his execution of deserters in the Creek War was murder.[17] Jackson imagined Clay's soiled hand behind every page of every document and bemoaned "the perfidy, the meaness, and wickedness, of Clay." To Sam Houston, now Tennessee's governor, he promised his enemy's "political, and perhaps, his actual destruction."[18]

John Overton initiated a strategy to answer the attacks: he formed the Nashville Central Committee, a pro-Jackson public relations operation that quickly prepared, published, and widely circulated materials responding to the attacks. Polk made himself available to research and draft documents to help counteract the anti-Jackson propaganda. From his boyhood in Maury County, he had heard about Jackson's violent temper. He worried now that these vicious blows on Old Hickory's character would prompt some vituperative outburst reinforcing the belief that he was an irresponsible hothead with an irrepressible temper.

The most painful blow to Jackson was a piece of "investigative reporting," initially published in a Cincinnati newspaper and reprinted in the anti-Jackson press, dredging up the events surrounding the "marriage" of Andrew and Rachel almost forty years earlier. It charged that the couple was guilty of bigamy and adultery. It was true that, around 1790, Andrew and Rachel had lived "in sin" for perhaps three years before she was legally divorced from the abusive Lewis Robards. John Overton, Jackson's intimate friend from those days, put together a plausible, if tortured, explanation for the Nashville Central Committee to circulate: the Jacksons, initially duped by Robards into believing she had been granted a divorce, remarried the moment they officially learned that the court had severed her marriage bond to her first husband. Rachel Jackson, now a near-religious zealot, died before her husband reached the White House. Jackson blamed Clay and the press for crushing her will to live.

Polk and Hugh Lawson White worked together to help the Nashville Central Committee answer other charges. They drafted an answer to the "murder" allegations relating to Old Hickory's decision to court-martial and execute deserting infantrymen. Polk pulled together depositions from soldiers who had served with Jackson, and documents from the War Department, all of which went into a voluminous report that was the basis for newspaper articles justifying every relevant action by the General. The old man expressed his deep gratitude by letter.

Polk now felt secure enough to write Jackson warning him to be cautious in his public statements. His enemies would not hesitate to pervert his plain English. Again, Jackson sent back a note of appreciation.

As election returns filtered in over a period of several weeks, the magnitude of Jackson's popularity, coupled with the public's resentment of Adams and Clay, had a powerful unifying effect on the country. Adams, as expected, carried his native area, New England, and ran ahead in New York. The smear campaign had failed, however; Jackson won 176 electoral votes to Adams's

83, and captured almost 647,000 popular votes to Adams's half million.

At home in Tennessee there was celebration from the Smoky Mountains to the Mississippi—none more enthusiastic than in the Duck River congressional district, where Polk turned out the voters to give Old Hickory a rout over Erwin's crowd.

3

Defender of the Faith

Once Jackson was safely elected, Adams ousted, and the American System—Clay's scheme to enlarge federal power—wrecked, Polk's posture in the House of Representatives changed. An attack-dog legislator during the Adams years, now he would become the protector and defender of the Jackson administration. As a freshman legislator in Tennessee, he had been the voice of Governor Carroll in the statehouse. In Congress, he would take on a similar role on behalf of the president.

Polk never trusted Jackson's closest friends, Senator John Eaton and William B. Lewis, but because they had been longtime supporters of the president and had worked tirelessly to elect him, the young congressman tolerated them. Lewis's role in the new administration must have been particularly obnoxious to Polk, the young idealist. When the sycophant was given the post as second auditor in the Treasury Department—the venue Jackson considered the largest cesspool of corruption—Polk thought the bandit had been given the keys to the bank.

At least the second auditor of the Treasury was a silent embarrassment. Eaton, as secretary of war, created a monumental public fiasco as his controversial marriage to Margaret O'Neale Timberlake escalated into a scandal that literally tore Jackson's cabinet apart.

THE EATON SCANDAL

The president had become fond of the attractive, ambitious young "Peggy" when he and Eaton came to Washington as senators in 1824 and lodged in her father's boardinghouse. After her husband, a naval officer, committed suicide at sea, snide gossip flew about the capital that Senator Eaton had "comforted" her in her "mourning." As Amos Kendall, a journalist and member of Jackson's kitchen cabinet, put it, "Scandal says they slept together."[1]

When Eaton told Jackson that he was thinking of marrying the recent widow, the president urged him to do so and they were wed on New Year's Day, 1829. To the wives of the other cabinet members, the new Mrs. Eaton was a scarlet woman. Led by Floride Calhoun, the vice president's wife, they shunned her, boycotted events if the Eatons were invited, and even refused Jackson's invitations to the White House.

President Jackson took it as a personal affront, scolded the cabinet members, and demanded that they force their wives to be kind to Peggy. The cabinet wives would not be forced.

Great silliness ensued. There came a time when the president actually canceled cabinet meetings for weeks on end. During this period, Polk and other Jackson supporters in Congress, who were fighting the president's battles against internal improvements, the Bank of the United States, high tariffs, and nullification, felt great frustration and longed for the stalemate to end. Sarah Polk, whose sympathies were with the cabinet wives, would not snub the Eatons but agreed with her husband that the place for her during this tense period was in Columbia.

The administration was a year old when Charles Wickliffe, Polk's House colleague from Kentucky, called a meeting to petition the president to fire the secretary of war. Wickliffe, a Calhounite, also wanted Jackson to fire Secretary of State Van Buren—who was unmarried and the only cabinet officer who had been courteous to Margaret Eaton. Polk never let Jackson know he had attended Wickliffe's meeting. All that came of it was an appeal for the president to resume cabinet meetings.

The Eaton scandal was but a prelude to Jackson's climactic break with Calhoun. Van Buren was doing all he could to create friction between the two men. Their friendship finally was severed when Jackson learned that Calhoun, as Monroe's secretary of war, had been critical in cabinet meetings reviewing Old Hickory's conduct during the expulsion of the Spaniards from Florida. Jackson confronted Calhoun and denounced him as a "most profound hypocrite."[2] The break was brutal and public. From the Capitol, Polk and his congressional colleagues had little advance warning of the sea change about to occur in government. Suddenly, Van Buren and Eaton resigned. Old Hickory demanded the resignations of the three cabinet officers who were Calhoun's close friends. Shortly afterward, another Calhoun supporter, the editor Duff Green, was discarded, and his *Telegraph* was replaced by a new paper, the *Globe*, edited by Kentuckian Francis Blair. The administration had new life, a new press voice—and old friends had become new enemies. The war inside the administration was over; the war in Congress over issues already had begun.

KNIGHT ERRANT

Trivialities and personalities disposed of, Polk and the other Jackson men in Congress were prepared to put their stamp of approval on the president's reforms. Opposition politicians were sniping away, and hostile newspapers were cartooning the cabinet officers who had resigned as rats fleeing a collapsing house.

The Buffalo-to–New Orleans road, first a controversial issue when Polk had run for the legislature, was an internal improvement project that appealed to many congressmen. Jackson wanted it killed—and Polk helped kill it. The latter recalled how his own constituents initially were "carried away" with the vagrant idea that the highway "was to run down every creek and pass through almost every neighborhood in the district."[3]

"The common sense of the people," however, finally took hold, Polk said. The "delusion passed off." Voters eventually realized that the project was calculated to "accumulate power" and create a "consolidated empire" dangerous to states' rights.[4] So the road bill went nowhere, because the road could not go everywhere.

There was, however, another internal improvement project that had a certain proposed destination. The Maysville road was drafted to run from Maysville, Kentucky, to Lexington, Henry Clay's hometown. The bill, far more than a piece of highway patronage for Kentucky's leading politician, required the federal government to buy stock in the private company that would construct and maintain the road. That, declared Jackson, was blatantly unconstitutional. To some congressmen, however, the road was necessary to allow the country to move westward. If Jackson was contemplating reelection (and, of course, already he was), why would he alienate the voters who favored the highway? Polk, acting on the president's urging, tied up the proposal for three long days of House debate. Polk argued that, far from being a national improvement, the Maysville road was a local highway for the sole benefit of Kentucky. To some members of Congress, he said, when a federal project promised to benefit their districts, "anything is national."[5] The debate ended, and the bill passed, 102 to 86. Jackson immediately vetoed it. His commitment was to protect the Constitution, he said, not fund pork barrel projects for congressmen, and he planned to pay off the national debt with the funds that would have built the road.

There were suspicions among Jackson's foes in Congress that Polk had been responsible for the strong language in the veto message. Polk insisted to his colleagues that the president was the true author. It was "emphatically his own . . . views."[6] The effort to override the veto failed, and from his Kentucky home, Clay, now

totally committed to running for president the following year, predicted that Jackson would pay a price for the veto at the ballot box in 1832. At the end of 1831, the Kentucky legislature sent Clay to the U.S. Senate knowing he was on his way back to the nation's capital to run for president.

Clay timed his arrival to coincide with his nomination for president by the anti-Jackson party, the National Republicans. Even in office, he was the most visible and vocal administration foe.

THE POLITICS OF NULLIFICATION

From his teenage years, Polk had seen General Jackson move from one controversy to another, making enemies along the way and keeping most of them. There were times when the president would work himself into a fit of temper at some newfound enemy when his young protégé found it difficult to share his antipathy. When the nullification issue arose over South Carolina's refusal to pay high tariffs, Jackson was in a rage. Calhoun, the father of the idea that tariffs imposed by the federal administration were in violation of the rights of states, maintained that South Carolina could declare its own authority over the federal government. Jackson saw such a refusal as a device to destroy his government's funding. More to the point, he was convinced that Calhoun's conclusion that a state could secede if it opposed a federal law threatened dismemberment of the Union.

Polk, a strong believer in states' rights, had mixed feelings about this issue. The tension between president and vice president was fierce, and Polk found himself tilting toward Calhoun's side of the scale. Early in the dispute between Jackson and Calhoun, Polk remained relatively aloof. Unlike Van Buren, who was out to undermine Calhoun and ingratiate himself with the president, he had little to gain from breaking off his friendship with the South Carolinian. After all, the Tariff of Abominations was as unfair to his Tennessee constituents as it was to Calhoun's in South Carolina. Polk

had come to recognize the South Carolinian as an astute political thinker with a substantial following among southern congressmen.

It was only when Calhoun took the long leap toward secession that Polk left the nullification train. Nullification was a first step toward disunion, and he was no secessionist. He supported Jackson's legislative response to South Carolina—the so-called Force Bill—that empowered the president to send troops, if necessary, to require a state's compliance with federal law. He also favored Jackson's initiative to lower tariffs, which helped cool the Calhounite passion to resist the tariff. The transition from sympathy toward Calhoun's nullification position to Jackson's force law was a huge leap—but having made it, he never again flirted with the thought that there was *any* right to secede.

THE BANK WAR

None of the intense struggles Polk undertook for Presidents Jackson and Van Buren while he was in Congress could match the protracted fury that attended the battle to kill off the Second Bank of the United States. It was here, in the bank war, that Polk, as a congressional investigator, moved another step closer to Jackson and, eventually, the presidency.

The conflict was personalized as a contest of wills between a president who would not be defied and a bank president who dared defy him. The question was whether the Jackson administration would oppose a rechartering of the bank in 1832, just as Old Hickory approached reelection. Nicholas Biddle, the bank's head, gambled that the president would not risk a move that seemed so unpopular. He had a good deal to learn about Jackson.

Polk's assignment from the president was to conduct a congressional investigation to expose the bank as an institution with the actual power to move the will of government against the best interests of the people, a parasitic corporation playing fast and loose with the people's money. Banks served a public purpose, but

the function of issuing paper notes was vital to the credit economy of the expanding nation. Banks held the monopoly on providing that credit. Polk's congressional probes would demonstrate that the government had no control over the monetary policy of the bank, could not make the institutions conform to administration policy, and that the government's money, in the vaults of the bank, was used to corrupt Congress and the press. Polk may have had the power to conduct a congressional inquiry to expose the bank's corruption, but Biddle had the wherewithal to wreak political as well as financial havoc. There would come a time when, feeling the pain of Polk's disclosures and Jackson's criticism, he would do just that.

Chartered in 1791, the First Bank of the United States was the brainchild of Alexander Hamilton, who candidly announced its elitist goal to "unite the interest and credit of rich individuals with those of the state."[7] Hamilton understood fully the potential of the institution: "Such a bank is more than a mere matter of private property, but a political machine of greatest importance to the state."[8]

The Second Bank came into being in 1816 with a twenty-year mandate and, like the First Bank, was the repository of federal funds, for which it paid the government no interest. Under Biddle's leadership, the Second Bank became a more effective political machine than ever before. Of the bank's twenty-five board members, only five represented the government, and Biddle kept them in the dark. One of them, Henry D. Gilpin, complained, "We know absolutely nothing. There is no consultation, no exchange of sentiments, no production of correspondence. . . . We are perfect cyphers."[9] In 1832, four years before the charter expired, Biddle—advised by Henry Clay—decided that this election year was the moment to press for a charter renewal. A credit economy had become a critical part of the fiscal policy of the nation. Democrats still insisted that gold and silver—specie—were the only valid currency, but paper notes, presumably backed up by specie in bank vaults, had rapidly become the tender of the times.

When Jackson began to rail against the bank as a monster to be slain—and told Van Buren, "The bank . . . is trying to kill me, but I will kill it"—Biddle armed his monster to do battle in the House and Senate.[10] Members of Congress suddenly were faced with a decision: they could follow a powerful and punitive bank president, with patronage favors and goodwill to dispense if his charter was renewed, or bow to a powerful and punitive president with his own supply of patronage and goodwill. It was a simple choice for Polk. For other congressmen, including John Bell from the Nashville district, it was a torturous decision. For one thing, he had inherited a family financial debt to Biddle's bank. For another, while he always had been considered a Jackson man, he was envious of Polk's standing with Old Hickory, and shortly thereafter the two younger men would become blood enemies. Bell was closer to Senator Hugh Lawson White than anyone else, and together they would one day upset Jackson's hold on Tennessee politics.

Repeatedly, as the bank war raged, the president would rely on Polk, first as a member of the Ways and Means Committee and then as its chairman, to expose the bank's corruption. He was up to the task, and his outspoken opposition to Biddle's institution gave him a measure of national prominence. When the Ways and Means Committee voted to approve the charter, Polk's stinging minority dissent won enthusiastic approval from the *Washington Globe*. His report's "facts and reasonings are perfectly irresistible. . . . It exposes the subterfuges . . . [of] that corrupt and corrupting institution in a manner so clear and convincing that it must satisfy every honest man."[11]

The *Globe*'s support of Polk did not deter Biddle. He pushed for an immediate vote, and the recharter bill passed 107 to 85, with Polk, of course, in the minority. Without blinking, Jackson vetoed it. Biddle knew he could not influence enough House members to override the veto, but he was not through. He continued to push, hoping the public would demand that the administration give him his way. The electorate was with Jackson and Polk and reelected them both. Van Buren became Jackson's vice president.

The president now decided to remove all federal money from Biddle's bank and deposit it in several state institutions, which become known as "pet banks." Polk, at Jackson's suggestion, was named chairman of the powerful Ways and Means Committee and produced a report that excoriated the bank, reciting a litany of justifications for removing federal deposits. Among the most serious: Biddle had excluded the government's directors from policy-making deliberations; he had put federal funds to his personal use; he had used the money to corrupt politicians and the press; he had impeded the government's efforts to pay down the national debt; he had used the power of the bank to influence the outcome of elections.

Of this last count, Polk had personal knowledge. Four days after his reelection to the House, he wrote to Francis Blair, editor of the *Globe*: "The influence of the bank on freedom of the press is visible in every quarter of the Union. . . . Even in Tennessee, it has its instruments, of which the *National Banner* at Nashville is the most prominent."[12]

He had discovered the *Banner* had engaged in what he called a journalistic "forgery" and "fraud" by publishing and circulating what purported to be an "Extra" edition of the *National Intelligencer* that praised the bank and damned Polk. He told Blair, "The whole power of the bank, through its organ [the *Banner*] was brought to bear on my Congressional District. . . . I was assailed through the *Banner*."[13]

He had no doubt that "the expense of publication was paid by the bank itself," which was "the real owner of the *National Intelligencer*."[14] Subsequent investigation documented Polk's charges. Biddle, in fact, had a personal hand in the "Extra" edition that had attacked Polk.

However adept Biddle was at banking, he was not a convincing editorialist. Polk carried his Duck River district with 70 percent of the vote. In the presidential contest against Clay, Jackson had swept to victory with 57 percent of the popular vote—688,000 ballots to 473,000. The electoral vote margin was 219 to 49. In Tennessee, Old Hickory crushed Clay, 28,000 votes to 1,400.

Still, the bank war raged on. The president came up with a new scheme to further discredit Biddle. He directed that all funds to pay veterans' benefits be taken from the bank and deposited in the "pet banks." When Biddle balked, Polk and Secretary of the Treasury Roger Taney blasted him for depriving veterans of their pensions.

Biddle, on the verge of losing the war, would not accept defeat. Jackson, he declared, had "scalped Indians and imprisoned judges" but would not "have his way with the bank."[15] He now unloaded a volley of blows to the economy, which historian Robert Remini described as devastating:

> Biddle . . . initiate[d] a general and strict curtailment of loans throughout the entire banking system . . . restricted bills of exchange, refused to increase discounts and ordered western banks . . . to purchase bills of exchange payable solely in eastern cities. . . . Throughout the fall months Biddle intensified his murderous squeeze. . . . The nation spiraled into recession and seemed headed into a major economic collapse.[16]

Biddle spurred a near panic. When a delegation of businessmen came to the White House to plead with the president for relief, he chastised them. "What do you come to me for . . . ? Go to Nicholas Biddle. Biddle . . . has millions of specie in his vaults . . . and yet you come to me to save you. . . . I tell you, gentlemen, it's all politics."[17]

It *was* all politics, and Biddle—even with Henry Clay and Daniel Webster on his payroll as lawyers—was out of his league. On the floor, Polk delivered a derisive indictment against him. The bank, he told his House colleagues, was despotic. If Biddle's power was not curtailed, he warned, no future president could come to office "without first making terms with the despot. It will control your election of President, of your Senators, and of your Representatives." It finally had come to this: "whether we shall have the republic without the bank or the bank without the republic."[18]

The *New York Courier and Enquirer*, the bible of the New York financial community, described it as "the most alarming speech that has been made to Congress for some years past."[19] John Quincy Adams, now a congressman from Massachusetts, had a different take on it. He wrote in his diary: "Polk has no wit, no literature, no point of argument, no gracefulness of delivery, no elegance of language, no philosophy, no pathos, no felicitous impromptus; nothing that can constitute an orator but confidence, fluency and labor."[20] He was better than that, but confidence, fluency, and labor were enough.

Jackson's supporters circulated Polk's speech across the country, and a broader audience began to take serious note of the Tennessee congressman. Back home, the president told the state's voters that Polk deserved a medal for his staunch fight for the people's interests.

THE FIRST DEFEAT

It was not a medal that Polk had in mind. Andrew Stevenson, the House Speaker, was about to resign and become minister to Great Britain. Polk wanted to succeed him. So did Congressman John Bell, who over the past years had drifted away from Jackson's camp. These two native sons of Tennessee would wrestle and claw each other for control of the House during three successive elections. Polk would win two out of three falls.

Their first battle came in 1834. Polk sorely needed the president's support to win, but William B. Lewis, Jackson's sycophantic crony, led him to believe that Old Hickory was cool to Polk's candidacy. Disappointment turned to elation when his brother-in-law James Walker, who was in Washington on business, found Jackson extremely receptive to the idea of Polk as the House's Speaker. "I am satisfied the old chiefs feelings are for you,"[21] he reported. By this time Polk already had received encouraging letters from Virginia, Ohio, North Carolina, and Alabama, and his friends Congressman Cave Johnson and Senator Felix Grundy were soliciting support from friends in Maine, New Hampshire, and New York.

So Jackson was still his hero. Vice President Van Buren, however, had his own ideas and favored Pennsylvania congressman Joel Sutherland. Calhoun's army of House nullifiers had their own candidate, Richard H. Wilde of Georgia. It would be a four-way race: Polk, Bell, Sutherland, and Wilde. From Nicholas Biddle's point of view, Polk was the enemy. Bell was his choice.

The exciting House election came in June, after Speaker Stevenson left for the Court of St. James. It was a seesaw affair involving ten rounds of voting. On the first ballot, Senator Calhoun's nullifiers threw all their weight to Wilde, and he led with 64 votes to Polk's 42; Sutherland had 34, Bell 30. When Van Buren saw Sutherland was a lost cause, he switched his support to Polk, who on the seventh ballot surged ahead with 83 votes, only 19 short of the majority. Bell, with Biddle's agents pushing him, had climbed to second place with 76. At that point Calhoun's nullifiers, determined not to let Van Buren have his way, shifted against Polk, and hurled every vote they could control to Bell. He forged ahead on the eighth ballot and won it on the tenth. Polk had lost his first election. Down Pennsylvania Avenue, Jackson, who had planned a feast to celebrate Polk's victory, was as dour as an undertaker. The doorman at the residence advised callers to stay away.

The combat between Polk and Bell went on for four more years, Polk turning the tables on him in December 1835 and ultimately winning the rubber match in September 1837.

Once he was Speaker, Bell was determined to become a king-maker. He had cut the cord to the Jacksonian political womb and knew it. Soon he would identify openly with Biddle and declare a need for the concept of *a* federal bank if not *the* Biddle bank. Jackson and Polk's supporters would criticize him sharply for that with his constituents back in Tennessee. In retaliation, and unhappy with the president's selection of Van Buren to succeed him as chief magistrate, Bell developed a strategy, with the support of other members of the Tennessee delegation, that would tear asunder Jackson's political control of the state.

With eleven members of Congress behind him, Bell importuned Senator Hugh Lawson White, one of Jackson's oldest friends, to run for president. To anyone outside Tennessee, it must have seemed a harebrained scheme with no chance of success. White, revered in Tennessee, was a respected senator, admired by many southern politicians, but he had no national following and no way to gain one. Van Buren had strong Democratic support from every part of the country. General William Henry Harrison, the hero at Tippecanoe, with Henry Clay's support, would run as a Whig, while Daniel Webster, the Senate lion from Massachusetts, had decided that this, at last, was the year he would permit the electorate to put him in the White House. In that competition, White's candidacy was what he once said of Jackson's 1824 race: a joke.

As for Bell, it is possible that he actually believed he could make White the candidate of the South and then, with help from Biddle, a national contender. He had told the banker that White, as chief magistrate, never would veto a bank charter bill. He was aware that his post as House Speaker was in jeopardy. He knew that Polk, with the president's support, would seek to unseat him in December 1835, just before the 1836 presidential election campaign. If he lost—and he would lose—he would have no influence with other members of Congress to help White or Biddle and his bank. Jackson saw through Bell's real strategy in encouraging White to run. He only sought to "secure his re-election to the speaker's chair, and recharter the United States Bank."[22]

Then, abruptly, Bell alienated the very members of the House whose support had elected him Speaker. He cut the congressional printing patronage contract from Duff Green, Calhoun's relative and closest friend, whose *United States Telegraph* was the voice of nullification. It was a self-inflicted wound. The nullifiers had helped elect Bell. Now they deserted him, and Polk won the 1835 Speaker's race 132 to 84.

In the presidential election the following year, the nation went for Van Buren, embracing Old Hickory's handpicked candidate with 764,000 votes—more than Harrison, White, and Webster combined. Van Buren carried fifteen states with 170 electoral votes. In Tennessee it was a different story. Polk managed to carry his district for Van Buren, but White, with growing Whig support at home, swept the state, 34,000 to 24,000. White also carried Georgia. His candidacy had one enduring effect. It gave a strong impetus to the building of a viable Whig party in Tennessee with the support of virtually half of the electorate. The days of Jacksonian dominance in the state had come to an end.

SPEAKER POLK

On December 7, 1835, Polk took the House Speakership from his newfound enemy, John Bell, and stood at the place where, a decade earlier, his archenemy, Henry Clay, had delivered the votes that sent John Quincy Adams to the White House. He must have felt a sense of satisfaction as he took the oath, but there was little time to reflect on his triumph. He was to preside over the Twenty-fifth Congress—the most sharply divided House in history, with 108 mostly loyal Democrats, 107 Whigs, and 24 members from scattered backgrounds: Anti-Masons, hard-line nullifiers, and equally hard-line Loco Focos, who saw themselves as advocates for the American underclass. These four years as Speaker would test Polk's toughness and try his patience. Beyond the divisions on issues, he knew there was a small clique of opponents already angling to unseat him in two years and return Bell to the job. Their strategy would be to hassle and harass him, attempting to make him appear as Van Buren's inept tool.

Polk would be the first Speaker to promote openly a president's agenda—which made him a lightning rod for the Whig opposition. As a freshman congressman, he had complained that the Adams administration had abused its power by rigging committee assignments to benefit the president. Now he embraced the very excesses he once condemned. He seeded every important committee with a Democratic chairman and a Democratic majority. He gave the nine-member Ways and Means Committee seven solid Democratic members. He named as the committee's chair Churchill Cambreleng, Van Buren's able and astute good friend from New York. He doled out some less important committees to opponents: John Quincy Adams, the former president, was given chairmanship of the Committee on Manufactures, and John Bell, his rival, became chairman of Indian Affairs. The bipartisan mask was transparent. Polk put it on for the sake of appearances, though it fooled no one.

Two issues, slavery and the economy, bedeviled him as he took the oath. The House resolution gagging debate on a stream of abolition petitions gave him the authority to muzzle heated discussion that too frequently included slashing insults and vituperative exchanges. Taking away the abolitionists' right of petition only served to further intensify the surly feelings that already interlaced partisan divisions in the House.

The economy could not be shoved under the House carpet. The Panic of 1837 was fast approaching. The tight money crunch Biddle instigated as he was about to lose the bank war had propelled a nationwide movement toward a new credit economy. State "pet banks" that received federal funds were issuing notes on land purchases, and suddenly there was a bloat of paper currency that mocked any pretense of fiscal prudence. Getting the government's money away from Biddle and into the pet banks had been like pulling teeth without novocaine, slow and painful, but many of those state institutions were now playing as fast and loose with the deposits as had Biddle. Senator Thomas Hart Benton groused, "I did not join in putting down the Bank of the United States, to put up a wilderness of local banks. . . . I did not join in putting down the paper currency of a national bank to put up a paper currency of a thousand local banks."[23]

Polk gave his constituents his sense of what had gone wrong. The nation had been seized by a "mania of speculation in lands, stocks, merchandise, Negroes, every description of property," he said. He related an anecdote to make his point. A young boy surprised his family when he rode home on a horse, and when asked by his father where he got the mount, the lad announced, "Why, I gave my note for him."[24]

It was paper trading in government land, mostly in the West, that was at the heart of the problem. Speculation in acreage was once more seen as the get-rich-quick panacea. It had started before Jackson left office as a growing infusion of banknotes fed the national appetite for limitless growth and triggered a dangerous price spiral. Old Hickory's departing executive order, the "Specie Circular," had been a "going away" present to Van Buren, designed to cure what was becoming galloping inflation. Since federal land sales were a centerpiece of the expansionist activity, this circular required that all future purchases of government property be transacted with hard money—gold or silver. After what Polk described as two years of "wild and extravagant overtrading . . . [with] irredeemable paper and rag money,"[25] the Panic of 1837 struck.

From 1834 to 1835, banknotes had increased from $95 million to $140 million, and the sale of public lands shot up from $4.5 million to $39.5 million.[26] The price of land, and just about everything else, including food, had skyrocketed. The middle class and working poor suffered most, but some hurting banks discontinued dealing in specie. Forced to surrender their federal deposits, some failed. At the Capitol, as at the White House, there was a public demand for action. Polk was hearing complaints from both his constituents back home and from members of the House, all of whom expected him to get President Van Buren to respond to the panic.

"Rescind the Specie Circular!" was the cry. Polk was unmoved by it. The circular had been Jackson's curative. From Nashville, the former president wrote Van Buren, urging him to ignore those pleas and give the circular a chance to work. To kill the circular would plunge the nation into deeper depression, he warned. Van Buren equivocated. Protest demonstrations developed in the East. The fledgling Loco Foco party, avowed enemy of banks and champion of the disadvantaged, pushed protest rallies in eastern states. A demonstration in New York transformed into a bloody riot over high food prices. It was not the only scene of volatile demonstrations— but the president, a New Yorker, always was sensitive to criticism from home.

Bankers poured into Washington to beg for an end to Jackson's evil circular. Polk was pressured not only by the lobbyists. John Bell was stirring up dissent in the House, seeking to use the Specie Circular to defeat Polk in the next Speaker's election.

Peter Temin's retrospective look at the Jacksonian economy found that "the Specie Circular itself did not have a great negative effect on the economy," and, in fact, it sent a positive message to the nation that the runaway inflation, propelled by paper notes, would end.[27] Those who were hurting, however, needed an immediate symbolic target, and the circular was it. Biddle's forces in Congress still had the idea that all would be well if fiscal control was returned to his bank. The pet banks now had congressional advocates arguing for a chance to cure the crisis. A new newspaper, the *Madisonian*, was created with the primary editorial policy of supporting state banks. After listening to his cabinet, Van Buren finally stayed with the Specie Circular, but in September 1837 he summoned a special session of Congress to deal with the economy, relying heavily on Polk's leadership to enact his program.

AN INDEPENDENT TREASURY

In the maelstrom, Van Buren revived an old idea whose time seemed to him to have come: an independent Treasury Department that would become the repository for all federal funds now deposited in private banks. Under the plan, the government would be the custodian of its own assets—specie, stored in fire-proof federal vaults, or "subtreasuries," as they were called. Bills would be paid and payrolls met by the administration from these funds. It would be a pox on both Biddle and the pet banks.

Looking ahead to his reelection campaign, Van Buren knew he needed to polish his image as a man of action. He thought the independent Treasury scheme would help do just that. Jackson sent word from the Hermitage that he strongly endorsed the plan. After much debate, the Senate, voting along party lines, passed the Independent Treasury Act 26 to 20.

Polk worked hard to get the needed House support, but the Whigs were united, determined to undermine any Van Buren initiative. Democrats, some influenced by patronage from either Biddle or the pet banks, were divided. Polk postponed the vote on the measure until the next session but still could not muster enough support for passage. He had recently beaten John Bell for a second time, 116 to 103. As recourse, Bell's backers opposed the Treasury bill, and with sixteen Democrats defecting, it went down to defeat, 125 to 111.

Ultimately, House members heard the voices of their constituents and passed the independent Treasury into law in June 1840—but without help from Polk. In 1838, he had finally succumbed to the prodding from Jackson, Grundy, Judge John Catron, Cave Johnson, and other leading Tennessee Democrats to resign and return home to run for governor. Polk was their best hope for reversing the Whiggish trend that had taken hold of Tennessee with White's 1836 presidential campaign.

Van Buren's concept of an independent Treasury had a short life. His loss of the presidency in 1840 meant the death of his initiative. The Tyler administration killed it in 1841 as Whigs, now in control of Congress, began to promote a return of federal funds to state banks. Henry Clay, never lacking in gall, still maneuvered for return to a Biddle-like national bank. Twice, in fact, his Whig lawmakers pushed his bank bills through—and twice Tyler vetoed them. For that and other lesser slights, Clay drummed Tyler out of the Whig party. It would be up to Polk, as president, to give the nation a permanent independent Treasury.

DISORDER IN THE HOUSE

Polk's years presiding over the House were stormy and, improbable as it seems, physically threatening. The experience hardened his emotional psyche and toughened his political hide. Unruly sessions frequently found him at the very edge of violence, with two of John Bell's confidants actually seeking to bait him into a duel.

Polk had seen how words uttered by politicians sometimes led to bloody tragedy. In 1830, during his third term in Congress, he rose to defend his then-friend Hugh Lawson White against a reckless allegation of bribery, leveled by a defeated Knoxville congressman, Thomas D. Arnold. "Base calumnies," said Polk of Arnold's charges—and for those words the defeated representative placed an ad in the *National Intelligencer* labeling Polk "a coward, a puppy, a liar and a scoundrel generally."[28] It was more than enough to provoke a challenge, but Polk ignored it. Two years later, in 1832, he defended his old friend Sam Houston, who had been charged with contempt of Congress after a street fight in which he viciously caned Ohio congressman William Stanberry into unconsciousness with a hickory stick. The catalyst: Stanberry had claimed on the

House floor that Houston was profiting from his relationship with Indian tribes. In February 1838, a trivial conversation between Congressman Jonathan Cilley, a Maine Democrat, and William Graves, a Kentucky Whig, led to a duel in which Henry Clay actually drafted the letter of challenge for Graves, who succeeded in killing Cilley with a rifle shot from eighty yards. It must have been chilling, then, for the Speaker to realize that Bell's friends were conniving to draw him into a duel.

For weeks on end, two congressmen, Bailie Peyton, a blustering Tennessean, and Henry Wise, a hot-tempered Virginian, let their plans be known. Both Polk's brother-in-law James Walker and his friend Cave Johnson picked up rumblings that Wise, known as "a dead shot" with a pistol, was determined to goad Polk into a challenge. Walker reminded him that it took "moral courage" not to respond.[29]

"There sat the Speaker like a cancer on the body politic," shouted Wise on one occasion. Polk, he said at another time, was guilty of "intriguing and subserviency" and of rigging the result of a committee investigation so as to make it meaningless. One day as Polk left the floor, Wise stood face-to-face with him and sneered that the Speaker was "damned arbitrary" and "a petty tyrant"; when Polk appeared unmoved by the insult, Wise blurted, "I mean it personal . . . damn you. Pocket it."[30]

When Representative Hopkins Turney, another Tennessee congressman, came to Polk's defense and accused Bell of fronting for Biddle and the bank, the ex-Speaker exploded, branding Turney a "scavenger of others—a tool of tools." Polk, he cried, was "as destitute of private honor as he was of private virtue."[31]

Suddenly, Bell and Turney came swinging at each other and had to be restrained. Polk required both to apologize to the House. When it was over, Bailie Peyton advised Bell to "load up those rifle barrell Pistols . . . which will kill a Buoffaloe." Shoot first, he counseled, at a distance of thirty yards, "aiming low, with a heavy charge." As to the Speaker, he suggested, "Pull Polk's nose on some pretext & get into a fight with him."[32] There was one major problem. Polk would not fight. In the face of verbal muggings from chronic critics, he was tempted to anger and sometimes his frustration showed, but he kept a tight rein on his temper. Jackson, the old gunslinger, sent word that he admired Polk's coolness in the face of verbal fire.

After Polk became president, Bell, Peyton, and Wise came on separate occasions to the White House bearing olive branches. Polk welcomed them all. When the president heard that Peyton worried that "past differences" would make their meeting awkward, Polk wrote in his diary he "had no unkind personal feeling towards Mr. Peyton, and that if he called upon him he would receive and treat him courteously and respectfully."[33] He did. His encounter with Wise was more formal. The "dead shot" from Virginia had become President Tyler's minister to Brazil. Polk inherited him and stood behind him when Wise gave a severe tongue-lashing to Brazilian officials who jailed a number of U.S. sailors in Rio de Janeiro. Polk kept the minister at his post even after Brazilians demanded his recall. A year later Wise came to Washington to thank Polk, who recorded in his diary, "I received him courteously. . . . I can never justify Mr. Wise's course at that time, but I . . . forgive it."[34] Bell, elected a Tennessee senator in 1847, was the last to make amends. He paid a courtesy call on Polk, who privately wrote, "I had not an unkind feeling towards him."[35] They agreed "to let bye-gones be bye-gones."[36] A decade and the aura of the presidency had tempered the loathing the three old enemies had held for their House Speaker.

HOME GROUND

In late 1837, that lingering ambition lodged at the core of his makeup stirred the Speaker of the House to look seriously at his chances to become president. At forty-two, Polk was young enough to bide his time, plan ahead, identify his options, and seize any moment that might move him toward that goal.

His present position, presiding over a divided House, fronting for an administration whose popularity was damaged by a hurting economy, was not an advantage. Moreover, no House Speaker in the almost six decades of the nation had been able to make the Speaker's desk a springboard to the White House—and history would decree that none after Polk would get there. He knew his position as Speaker was precarious. Whigs were gaining national momentum and might soon have a controlling majority in the House, in which case he would be deposed.

His best option, he decided, was to go home to Tennessee, run for governor, take that office away from the Whigs, and restore Jacksonian democracy to the state that had given it to the nation. He and Jackson would work to convince Van Buren that his presidential reelection prospects in 1840 would be markedly enhanced if he dumped aging Vice President Richard M. Johnson as a running mate and urged the Democratic convention to nominate Governor Polk. It would be an attractive ticket, combining North and South with two proven moderates, both wedded to the tradition of Jefferson and Jackson.

The governor's race, however, would not be easily won. Four years earlier, Newton Cannon had thumped Billy Carroll by 11,000 votes to win the office, and then two years later enlarged his margin to 17,000 over Jackson's old friend Robert Armstrong. Reversing the Whig trend and defeating Cannon would require an exhaustive effort by Polk.

He went at it in typical style. The quintessential micromanager, he personally laid out his campaign strategy. His initial step was to establish a solid link with the Tennessee nullifiers, who were close to Calhoun but had nothing to gain from supporting Governor Cannon or Henry Clay's party. At the same time, he worked to recruit viable Democratic congressional candidates in each of the twelve districts. He designed a backbreaking tour covering the state's 550-mile expanse, from the mountains of upper East Tennessee to Memphis in the west, inviting Cannon to join him for a series of speeches.

At the same time he sought to enliven the interest of the editors of the state's Democratic newspapers, using the *Nashville Union,* which he had helped found, as his primary news organ. The Whig press was hostile to his return. The *Memphis Enquirer* editorialized that "the democracy in this state is dying a violent death and Mr. Polk is dispatched as a Democratic physician extraordinary with violent palliatives and a new batch of nostrums. . . . But our people will not swallow them."[37] The *Paris West Tennessean* described Polk as "artful, cunning, intriguing" but warned readers: "he is a snake in the grass."[38]

The two candidates officially began the race with a joint appearance in Murfreesboro on April 11, 1839. The historian Robert White encapsulated the events:

> Polk proved himself a skillful debater, a master of repartee and ridicule and by the end of the month Governor Cannon announced that the duties of his office rendered it imperative that he discontinue the joint campaign. . . . Late in the campaign Cannon announced . . . engagements in East Tennessee. . . . Polk joined Cannon and trod on his toes until the end.[39]

On Election Day the result was hairline close: Polk, 54,012; Cannon, 51,396—a margin of only 2,616 out of more than 105,000 votes cast.[40] By anybody's count, it was a remarkable victory; 20,000 Tennesseans who two years earlier had voted for Cannon now cast their ballots for Polk.

Polk's inaugural was equally impressive, attended by reinvigorated Democrats, Old Hickory himself making the trip from the Hermitage to pay tribute to his young protégé. The old man's pride must have swelled as Polk announced that his administration would regulate state banks, improve education, provide state-financed internal improvements, and support the cause of the citizen against corporate power.

Polk's two years as governor did not live up to the promise. The deep recession that was damaging Van Buren's administration dragged down Polk's agenda. His three major programs, regulating state banks, implementing state internal improvements, and upgrading education, all failed to get legislative approval. The state's bank directors had mismanaged its affairs, and, as White wrote: "Banking . . . held the Legislature in a straight jacket for practically the entire session. . . . Financial quack doctors, some of whom were members of the Legislature, displayed their cure-alls and panaceas."[41]

Notably, there also was "a veritable medley of 'spirits' bills that clogged the legislative hopper."[42] The lawmakers were willing to regulate liquor, if not the banks. In the end, the state financial problems defeated Polk's hopes for improving Tennessee. Funds could not be found to improve schools or push for necessary infrastructure improvements. Defections among Democratic legislators, heavily influenced by the banking lobby, knocked out Polk's plan to regulate banks.

The partisan cleavage he had left in Congress was equally pervasive in the state legislature, but Democrats at home held a narrow advantage in both houses. Polk managed to appeal to the majority's party loyalty and maneuver the general assembly to unseat the two sitting Whig U.S. senators, the beloved Hugh Lawson White and the respected Ephraim Foster. From the distance of Nashville, Polk sent Van Buren two new Democratic senators, demonstrating to the president just how effective a vice president he could be. The governor called on his old mentor-at-law, Attorney General Felix Grundy, now serving in Van Buren's cabinet, to fill White's seat, and picked a fallen Whig, Alexander Anderson, from Knoxville, to succeed Foster.* The legislature voted along strict party lines. It was a victory for

---

*Grundy died in office thirteen months later. Polk supported A. O. P. Nicholson as his successor.

raw partisanship in a two-year administration that saw few other achievements.

Throughout his term as governor, Polk found himself repeatedly needled by a thirty-year-old freshman lawmaker from Wilson County, James C. Jones. Tall and gangling (he was six feet and weighed but 125 pounds), "Lean Jimmy" Jones would turn out to be more a thorn in Polk's career than a prick in his legislative programs. Jones was a legislative voice for religionists who sought to close tippling houses, and built a constituency by proposing laws to provide support for the families of men afflicted by "intemperance." He also sponsored the law for a state "Lunatic Hospital." As Polk's reelection campaign neared, the Whigs picked Jones to challenge the sitting governor.

Lean Jimmy was an unconventional but effective campaigner. Polk had contended with great lawyers like Felix Grundy in the courtroom and the state legislature, and debated with John Quincy Adams, Edward Everett, and Henry Wise in Congress. But he never had met the likes of an adversary like Lean Jimmy Jones, whose style of debate included "ridicule, sarcasm, wit, buffoonery and a deluge of epithets."[43] It was great theater but hardly uplifting, since Jones rarely permitted facts to obscure his points; for example, he argued that the Whig position in favor of high tariffs lowered the cost of consumer goods. The historian Charles Sellers wrote that, on the stump, Jones "maintained such an air of courtesy and magnanimity that an opponent could not attack the absurdities of his arguments without arousing sympathy."[44] Polk remarked that he might do better if, in their frequent face-offs, he "borrow[ed] Jones' joke book."[45]

The outcome was no joke. It was yet another close race, with Polk losing by 3,243 votes after 103,900 ballots had been cast. There was one marked difference in the election returns: the Calhoun nullifiers in eastern Tennessee, having observed Polk's continued affection for Martin Van Buren, stayed home, and Polk, who had lost that area of the state by only 361 votes against

Cannon, now was beaten there by 3,223. Van Buren cost him the election.

But Polk had the vice presidency in mind, and as delegates gathered for the 1840 Democratic convention, his name was floated against the incumbent, Richard M. Johnson of Kentucky, the heralded slayer of Tecumseh. Johnson had fathered two daughters by a slave woman, and many delegates were ambivalent about him—but Polk was now a loser. When it became clear to Polk that neither he nor Johnson could get enough delegates to win the nomination, he withdrew his name. He would go home, he decided, rally the Democracy one more time, and vie again with Lean Jimmy Jones for the governorship.

In Tennessee, Polk was still the leader of the party; but, denied the power of the governor's office, he had little to rely on but those deeply rooted partisan instincts that drove him to try to curb the power of the opposition. It was another close election, and Jones defeated him. The voters divided the state legislature, giving the senate to the Democrats and the house to the Whigs.

When Jones and the Whigs sought to elect two new U.S. senators to replace Nicholson and Anderson, whose terms had expired, the Democrats designed an unsophisticated but successful strategy to block them; the thirteen Democrats in the state senate simply refused to come together to vote, leaving their twelve Whig colleagues powerless without a quorum, and the U.S. Senate seats vacant. On no fewer than seventy-two occasions over many months the "immortal thirteen" Democrats, as the friendly party press called them, refused to vote. President Van Buren was delighted not to have to deal with two more Whigs in the Senate, but many voters in Tennessee were outraged.

Polk felt the sting of voter anger at the polls, losing to Jones by a margin of 3,833 with more than 110,000 votes cast. It was a scant change—a 610-ballot difference—from the outcome two years earlier. Polk was seized by a sense of failure. He had failed to restore Jacksonian Democracy to Tennessee. He would pin his hopes on becoming a viable vice presidential candidate in 1844, and on joining forces with Van Buren to provide the winning ticket. Deep in his partisan soul, though, he must have felt what everybody thought. He was through.

4

Another Bargain

In early May 1842, the two sworn political foes—clearly at that moment the nation's most prominent and prestigious politicians—Martin Van Buren, former president, and Henry Clay, former secretary of state and former U.S. House Speaker, met at Ashland, Clay's graceful Kentucky manse just outside Lexington.

Van Buren was on a tour of the South, a region where he was too little understood and too much disliked, hoping to improve his image. Immediately before visiting Clay, Van Buren had stopped off to see Polk and Jackson at the Hermitage in Tennessee. These were two markedly different meetings: one open and trusting with warm friends; the other guarded and cautious with a frosty, if affable, rival. The New Yorker had billed his tour as "nonpolitical," a claim that was ludicrous. He politicked at every stop, including Nashville, Columbia, and Lexington, where, incidentally, Kentucky Democrats threw a bash for him at the end of his stay with Clay.

The mere fact that Van Buren and Clay sat down together for most of a week was historically notable. James K. Polk arguably never would have become the eleventh president had the unlikely meeting between the two old enemies not occurred. Two years later, on the same day, in separate Washington newspapers, Van Buren and Clay announced simultaneously their opposition to annexing the independent Republic of Texas. For the foreseeable future, they concluded, bringing Texas into the Union was unwise. That was a position that defied powerful public opinion—and it launched Polk's presidential candidacy.

Despite the best efforts of Clay and Van Buren to make it appear that they spent their time together chatting idly about everything from the weather to the Saxony sheep raised at Ashland, their meeting was charged with drama. Over many years Clay and Van Buren had insulted, criticized, and castigated each other in public speeches and private correspondence. Now it was a virtual certainty that they would soon be coldly partisan opponents in a heated contest for the presidency—the New Yorker as the nominee for Jackson's Democratic party; Clay as the candidate of the Whig party he had founded. Polk, who would steal the nomination away from Van Buren and go on to beat Clay for the presidency, was not remotely thought of by either of them. Van Buren was cool even to the idea of Polk running as his Democratic vice presidential candidate.

Clay and Van Buren coveted the presidency. Van Buren had won it in 1836 and lost it four years later; Clay had run for it in 1824 and 1832, and twice had been denied this holy grail. They both were aging, and, realistically, this would be their last real chance. And so the clichéd axiom once again held true: Politics makes strange bedfellows.

Historians still disagree on whether Clay and Van Buren entered into an agreement, while at the Kentuckian's home, to separately and simultaneously come out against U.S. annexation of Texas.* When their statements were published in April 1844,

*Robert Remini noted in his biography of Jackson that he was convinced the two candidates cut the deal on Texas while at Ashland. Later, in his biography of Clay, he wrote that after reconsidering the matter he had concluded that no such bargain was struck, and candidly asserted that his original finding was wrong. He relied on letters written by Clay immediately after Van Buren left Lexington and on his considered opinion that Clay, having been burned by the "corrupt bargain" of 1824, would have been too wary to risk striking another bargain on Texas.

they were accused of "striking an agreement."[1] They denied it. Politics was their shared passion. Each held himself out to be a gentleman, and, as among thieves, there was a code of honor between them. What was said at Ashland would stay at Ashland.

Clay respected Van Buren's fiction that his trip to the South was nonpolitical, and reported to friends immediately after Van Buren headed back east that "not much politics" was discussed.[2] It did not take "much politics" to get around to their shared interest in keeping the issue of slavery out of their campaigns. At that moment in the nation's history, there were thirteen slave states and thirteen states where the institution was outlawed. If the two candidates allowed Texas annexation to become an issue in their contest, it well might become the only issue. There would be an immediate, prolonged, and passionate debate over whether the new state should be slave or free. Clay and Van Buren could agree that the nation, and their campaigns, should be spared that.

During the meeting at the Hermitage, there was no pretense on the part of Jackson and Polk that they would not talk politics with Van Buren. The New Yorker had not seen Old Hickory since 1837, when he had succeeded Jackson in the White House. The welcome he received from his old leader was affectionate. They all understood why Van Buren had come south, and no doubt Henry Clay was raked over the political coals as the three Democratic leaders explored strategies to defeat him.

At Columbia, Polk rallied thousands of Democrats for a "nonpolitical" reception, obviously intended to show Van Buren that he and Polk were popular and together could carry Tennessee.[3] Polk reported afterward that neither he nor Jackson raised the question of his vice presidential candidacy. Van Buren gave no hint as to what he would do about a running mate. He certainly did not indicate to either of his Tennessee hosts that he would oppose Texas joining the Union. That would have brought an eruption from Old Hickory. Van Buren had heard Jackson say with the fervor of a biblical prophet, "The god of the universe . . . intended this great valley [Texas] to belong to one nation."[4]

TYLER'S OFFER

In the weeks before the Democratic convention, Polk's closest friends, Congressmen Cave Johnson and Aaron Brown, began to feel out his prospects to run for vice president on Van Buren's ticket. Polk craved their gossipy reports, even asking Cave to scold Aaron for not writing more frequently with news of his prospects. Johnson reported that the Ohio convention had endorsed Van Buren over Senator Lewis Cass of Michigan, his only real challenger for the presidency, but the delegates had failed to take a stand on the vice presidential nomination—though both former vice president Richard M. Johnson of Kentucky and Senator William Rufus King of Alabama were mentioned ahead of Polk. Virginia, according to Aaron Brown, "will give the vice [president] the go by."[5] Mississippi endorsed Van Buren and Polk over Cass and King, Cave Johnson said. Brown's sources reported that while Polk and King were "disputing" about the vice presidency, Richard Johnson might snatch the second spot on the ticket away from both of them. Cass backers were circulating a report, Brown said, that the Michigan candidate favored Polk as his running mate. Be careful with this information, he warned. It was a trap to bring Polk's friends to Cass, but it certainly would make Van Buren backers think Polk was disloyal to their man. Brown and Johnson concluded that Cass simply did not have the votes to beat Van Buren, so they had no hope but to stay with the former president. The rumors flew.

All of them felt distress and dejection at the Whig party's ascendancy. The two Tennessee congressmen believed, at this point, that Van Buren represented the Democrats' best hope to regain the White House. But they also knew that the former president looked upon Polk as a twice-defeated governor, rather than a political star whose presence on the ticket would add buoyancy to the party's aspirations. They understood that Polk's strained and wishful effort to become vice president well might be his last hurrah.

At home in Columbia, as he read correspondence and press reports from across the country, it seemed to Polk that, while Van Buren clearly was the favorite, every Democratic leader with any reputation—Lewis Cass of Michigan, John Calhoun of South Carolina, James Buchanan of Pennsylvania, Thomas Hart Benton of Missouri, Levi Woodbury of New Hampshire, even former vice president Richard Johnson—had some faint hope that lightning would strike and make him the party's nominee. Yet it was clear that, absent some convention upheaval, Van Buren would take the nomination.

If the former president had a preference for his running mate, he kept it to himself. Richard Johnson was a candidate largely as a result of self-promotion; the boomlet for Senator William Rufus King of Alabama was engineered primarily by his roommate, Senator James Buchanan of Pennsylvania.

As anxious and preoccupied as Polk was about the nomination, he also was now challenged for the symbolic leadership of the Democratic party in Tennessee. A. O. P. Nicholson, a bright, brash, driven young man from the Duck River district whom Governor Polk had ordained as a U.S. senator, was a mercurial personality. Without consulting with Polk, he was cozying up to Cass, sending a message to Polk that should the Michigander become president, Nicholson, not Polk, would be the new titular head of the Tennessee Democratic party. At one point Polk compared Nicholson's disloyalty to Bell's earlier betrayal. "I would prefer . . . an open opponent, to a hypocritical friend in disguise," he said.[6]

There was more than Nicholson's perfidy to distract Polk from his vice presidential efforts, although making the race with Van Buren was never off his mind for long. On the last day of February 1844, Aaron Brown wrote with tragic, if exciting, news from

Washington: "That confounded new steam ship the *Princeton* has played the wild today. Her big gun bursted"[7] during an at-sea demonstration of a gigantic new naval weapon, the Peacemaker. The explosion killed Secretary of State Abel Upshur, Secretary of the Navy Thomas Gilmer, Commodore Beverly Kennon, and David Gardiner, a wealthy lawyer and father of Julia Gardiner, the lovely young woman President Tyler would soon marry. Ten days after the Peacemaker tragedy, Polk received a surprising invitation. President Tyler wanted him as the new secretary of the navy, succeeding Gilmer. Aaron Brown and Cave Johnson, believing the vice presidency was becoming a remote possibility for Polk, urged their friend to take the cabinet job. Polk, however, was obstinately set on his dreams. "If I ever again filled any public place," he said, it would be by vote of the people.[8] By the time he learned that he was Tyler's second choice for the post, he had already declined.

The *Princeton* explosion jolted President Tyler into action. Suddenly, he began performing as an incumbent president who was running for reelection. Within ten days after the tragedy, he had picked John C. Calhoun, a staunch pro-slavery voice, to succeed Upshur as secretary of state, filled the navy job with John Y. Mason, one of Polk's North Carolina schoolmates, and sent Senator King off to be minister to France, removing him from the vice presidential picture.

The president then set his sights on immediately bringing Texas into the Union. Earlier he had asked Daniel Webster, then his secretary of state, "Could anything throw so bright a lustre around us?"[9] Webster dissuaded him at the time, fearing that any effort to take Texas into the Union would create a backfire of controversy over slavery and hurt the administration. Now, with the death of Upshur, Calhoun was secretary of state and strongly in favor of bringing in Texas as a slave state. He urged Tyler to take action on this issue, and, on April 12, 1844, the president sent the Senate a resolution calling for the annexation of Texas as the twenty-seventh state.

It was the last thing Van Buren or Clay wanted. Each was preparing to come out against annexation, and they used their influence with both Democrats and Whigs in the Senate to quickly defeat the proposal. It died ten days later by a vote of 35 to 16.

THE TEXAS QUESTION

Four days later—and twenty-three months after their summit at Ashland—Clay and Van Buren published their separate, "coincidental" statements against Texas annexation: Clay's in the *National Intelligencer*, Van Buren's in the *Globe*. The news hit Washington like a verbal meteor that, as Robert Remini described it, "sent shock waves across the country."[10]

A day later, on April 27, 1844, word from the nation's capital reached Tennessee. Polk, still clinging to a thread of hope that Van Buren would support him for the vice presidential nomination, was jolted. Only five days earlier, he had mailed to a Cincinnati Democratic club a statement of what he thought was party doctrine. "I am in favor of the immediate re-annexation of Texas to the territory and Government of the United States," he had written.[11] Imagine his vexation on discovering that he and Van Buren, the man whose candidacy he wanted to embrace, were in disagreement.

It is astonishing that Clay and Van Buren, astute, cunning, veteran politicians, so misread the public mood. Texas, for most residents of the United States, was a natural extension of the nation. Nearly everyone had family, friends, or former neighbors there. The population had soared to more than one hundred thousand that year.

Everybody remembered the Mexican slaughters of innocents at the Alamo and Goliad. With pride, they remembered that Sam Houston had avenged those outrages and won independence for Texas at the Battle of San Jacinto. There was a line on maps that separated the United States from the Republic of Texas, but, whatever the politicians said, public sentiment already had annexed Texas.

Both Van Buren and Clay may have isolated themselves from public opinion, but they were not thoughtless. They both needed and expected to get votes, from both the North and the South. If they allowed Texas to become the major campaign issue, rabid pro-slavery forces would demand that both candidates promise that, as president, they would support slavery in the new state. On the other side, fiery leaders of the abolitionist movement would insist that Van Buren and Clay declare support for making Texas a free state.

At the time, slavery was a reasonably manageable political issue, with exactly half of the twenty-six states still permitting slavery and the other half barring it. Over many years in public life these two men had crafted carefully worded statements on the subject that were acceptable to most voters in all parts of the country. Their positions—like that of Polk—were considered moderate, middle of the road, acceptable to masses of people in the North and South. Clay, a slaveholder, had said that the institution should end, and that when it did he would sell his slaves. That was for consumption in the North. He also predicted it would disappear gradually. Southerners heard that as "perhaps never." As a young man, Van Buren had inherited a slave who escaped, and he never again owned a human being. Yet he was no abolitionist; he never could have been elected president in 1836 had he been. He satisfied those who opposed slavery by standing against its extension to other states—and placated southerners by favoring the status quo, leaving the matter up to the determination of each state. Thus both were viewed as candidates who would not rock the slavery boat. Polk's position was closer to Van Buren's than to Clay's. A slaveowner throughout his life, Polk, like Clay, had branded the institution as "evil." It was not a statement he often repeated. After he became president, his position on

Texas and slavery was that it was a matter for citizens of the new state to decide—which meant for white, male Texans to decide. Both Clay and Van Buren, during their tenures as secretary of state, had tried to buy Texas from Mexico. The Mexicans had been insulted when President Adams authorized Clay to offer $1 million for the territory, and reacted the same way when President Jackson told Van Buren to raise the proffer to $5 million.

To complicate the issue, President Tyler, a Democrat-turned-Whig who was now acting again more like a Democrat, continued to push Congress for immediate annexation. He hoped it might be the issue that could keep him in the White House. Public support strongly was with Polk, Jackson, and Tyler—and against Clay and Van Buren.

Two weeks after Van Buren's statement was published, Cave Johnson wrote, "I am sick of this place & these things & am almost tempted to resign in disgust . . . quit politics forever."[12]

When Jackson got wind of what Van Buren had done, he knew instantly that the New Yorker never again would be president. After shedding "tears of regret," Old Hickory wrote Van Buren a brutally frank letter. There was as much chance for him to be elected, said Jackson, as there was "to turn the current of the Mississippi."[13]

Van Buren could only pray that the old man was wrong. He was still the leading candidate for the nomination. He counted heads and calculated that, even with the defections resulting from his stand against Texas annexation, he still had a comfortable margin to win the Democratic nomination, including the backing of James K. Polk. Van Buren would send his supporters off to the Baltimore convention with full confidence that he had a committed majority. A majority would not be enough.

THE CENTER OF THE ACTION

Baltimore was the country's political center that year. The Whigs gathered there on May 1 for their convention, with the Democrats arriving in town on the twenty-seventh. Tyler, not ready to give up his life in the White House, convened his own party, the newly minted Democratic-Republicans, in the same city on that same day. His was an unambiguous message to Jackson's party, now angrily divided over the Texas controversy. Tyler, despite his recent Whig past, hoped to become a viable Democratic candidate. The internecine divisions in the party just might give him a chance to be their choice, if he could stay in the action.

Baltimore's proximity to Washington made it the ideal venue for the conventions. The Whigs, bursting with confidence, gathered at the Universalist church on Calvert Street and settled their business with vigor and haste, while Clay waited forty miles away in the nation's capital for the unsurprising news that he was his party's choice. Not a single Whig seemed to care about Clay's stand on Texas. They had waited too long for the chance to put in place the Whigs' great American System, with its promise of internal improvements, protective tariffs, the return of a single federal bank, and the rebirth of a full economy. The convention exploded with ringing shouts and joyous clamor at the mention of Clay's name, and he was unanimously nominated. It took three ballots to select Theodore Frelinghuysen of New Jersey as his running mate. The Whigs went back to their home states unified and confident.

On the twenty-seventh, Tyler's crowd, primarily made up of federal workers with a day off, met at Calvert Hall. Rallying around their only major campaign plank, *Tyler and Texas*, the Tylerites managed to work up almost as much enthusiasm for their president as the Whigs had for Clay.[14] The president's nomination was flashed to Washington via the new Morse code telegraph, and Tyler wired back his already prepared acceptance. Aside from his wedding two weeks later, this was the only thing the president could celebrate during his remaining ten months in office.

The Democrats, in contrast, gathered at Odd Fellows Hall on North Gay Street with a marked undercurrent of despair. Their confidence in Van Buren had been shaken by his declared opposition to annexing Texas. Many feared that open campaign warfare between nullifiers and abolitionists, now almost certain in the wake of Van Buren's Texas stand, would destroy the party. Van Buren still controlled a majority of the delegates, but his support was softening. If an alternate candidate arose, the convention could be thrown into chaos. A small clique of Tennesseans, however, had devised a scheme that would launch the nation's first "dark horse" presidential candidate.

Just two weeks earlier, Polk and Robert Armstrong, the Nashville postmaster, were summoned to the Hermitage to plot with Jackson and Andrew Jackson Donelson, Old Hickory's nephew and confidant. After those two weeks of agony over Van Buren's rejection of Texas, Jackson had concluded that it would lead to disaster and defeat if Van Buren should win the nomination. He had just drafted another statement to be published before the convention, yet another devastating wound to Van Buren. The old man had faith that when Van Buren realized his mistake and understood that his cause was hopeless, patriotism would lead him to withdraw. It would be imperative to have another candidate in place to save the party, Jackson told his visitors. They must prepare to nominate Polk for president.

Handling the Van Buren crowd would not be easy. Polk immediately wrote to Cave Johnson, saying that Van Buren's friends "will probably hold the balance of power and will be able to control the nominations for both offices, and therefore the great importance of conciliating them."[15] He further reported to Cave:

> Gen. J. says the candidate for the first office should be an annexation man, and from the Southwest, and he and other friends here urge that my friends should insist upon that point. I tell them, and it is true, that I have never aspired so high and that in all probability the attempt to place me in the first position would be utterly abortive. In the confusion that will prevail . . . there is no telling what will occur.[16]

It may have been uncharacteristic modesty that led Polk to question Jackson's judgment in recommending him for the presidency. In his own mind, he was convinced the party would pick a man "from the north." Nonetheless, he decided, it would leave him in a "favorable position . . . for the vice presidential nomination. I aspire to the 2nd office."[17]

Polk would rely heavily on Cave Johnson as his eyes and whispered voice in the volatile political cauldron that would be Baltimore. His friend would need help, of course, and four stalwart allies were on the way to assist Cave and Aaron Brown. Even as Polk wrote Johnson, Sam Laughton, editor of the *Union*, Donelson, Gideon Pillow, Polk's former law partner, and William Childress, his wife's cousin—-all convention delegates —were bound for Baltimore, drafted into the game plan that Jackson had outlined to save the Democratic party.

Polk had his own strategies for the convention. Having presided over a Congress torn by dissension, he knew how difficult it would be to harmonize the delegates after Van Buren fell. Cave Johnson and Aaron Brown would be more successful, he deduced, if they avoided the jaded Washington crowd and solicited support from among the delegates arriving "fresh from the people." As these "people delegates" rolled into the capital en route to Baltimore, Polk advised Johnson and Brown to take them aside and persuade them to "take the matter into their own hands, to control and overrule their leaders in Washington. . . . The Delegates from a distance alone can do this."[18]

Polk's political savvy could be seen in the details of his letter to Johnson: Bring just one delegate from every state, he suggested, to a meeting at Washington's Brown Hotel before they departed for the convention. Explain to them that the survival of the party was at stake. Move cautiously, he directed, "without announcing to the public what you are at."[19] It was an ingenious tactic. When these delegates observed the acrimony inside Odd Fellows Hall, their preconvention briefing would take hold. Polk urged Johnson to share the letter confidentially with Gideon Pillow, one of Tennessee's most able lawyers, in whom he had great confidence. Since Polk's first campaigns for Congress, Pillow had been his loyal friend. Together they had supported Van Buren in 1840 when other Tennessee Democrats defected to Hugh Lawson White. Pillow was shrewd, Polk told Johnson, and could be a crucial ally and leader.

Unrest and discontent pervaded the convention even as the delegates were gathering that morning. A Cass delegate, Romulus Saunders of North Carolina, climbed to the podium without permission before all the delegates were in the hall and proposed that Hendrick Wright, a Pennsylvanian, be named convention chair. A chorus of "ayes" carried, and the Van Buren forces had lost the first round even before the bell rang. Saunders immediately tried to shove through another anti–Van Buren measure: the two-thirds rule, which would require that a candidate receive the votes of two-thirds of the 266 delegates to win the party's mantle. Cave Johnson leaped to his feet to stop the Cass steamroller before it took over the convention. He shouted out that the motion was premature; delegates had not even been seated or certified.

It was a smart move on Johnson's part. It sent a message to Silas Wright, Benjamin Butler, and Azariah Flagg, heading the New York delegation for Van Buren, that Polk's friends were looking out for their interests. It made no difference, of course. The two-thirds rule was adopted the next day by 32 votes, 148 to 116. Some delegates who were pledged for Van Buren, but were unenthusiastic about him, voted for it knowing that they were crippling his candidacy. Van Buren would lead the balloting when it began, but with the two-thirds rule, he could not win.

Behind the scenes, events were taking place that would upset both Van Buren's and Cass's strategies. Gideon Pillow, exercising that shrewdness Polk attributed to him, struck up an alliance with George Bancroft of Massachusetts. Bancroft, a distinguished historian who loved politics, had long been a Van Buren man, but his alliance with Pillow would make the ultimate difference for Polk. They agreed that Polk's candidacy was not to be openly pursued until it was clear that Van Buren would lose. The two conspirators noted the open hostility between the Cass and Van Buren camps. For Polk to have a chance, Bancroft and Pillow had to keep both sides friendly, and there had to be a scattering of votes for other candidates.

On the second morning of the convention, the balloting began. At the end of the first roll call Van Buren had 146 votes—a clear majority, but 31 shy of the two-thirds needed. Cass had 83. Five other candidates received votes: former vice president Johnson, 24; Calhoun, 6; Buchanan, 4; Levi Woodbury, 2; Charles Stewart, 1. No one had mentioned James K. Polk.

Both Pillow and Bancroft later would claim credit for Polk's success, and clearly each had an important role to play. Bancroft, aided by Massachusetts governor Marcus Morton, quietly moved among northern party men, encouraging them to support Polk if Van Buren's candidacy collapsed. Pillow used the same soft approach with selected southern delegates. Simultaneously, Cave Johnson advised Silas Wright, the popular senator from New York, that the Tennessee delegation would be prepared to support him for the nomination if Van Buren stepped aside. As Speaker of the House, Polk had worked with and respected Wright, but this was a move designed to promote good feelings with the battered New York delegation. Wright, as expected, rebuffed Johnson. He would decline any move to nominate him, out of loyalty to Van Buren.

The timing of the Polk strategists was impeccable. They had to overcome a move by Buchanan backers, who were soliciting some of the same delegates, hoping to make the Pennsylvanian the compromise candidate.

A second roll call of the states began almost immediately. The two-thirds rule had a disabling effect, and Van Buren's support plummeted to 127. By the fourth roll call, Cass had forged ahead of the former president by 4 votes. By the seventh, Cass led 123 to 99. The other minor candidates wilted in the heat.

There still had been no official word about Polk, but off the floor his name was whispered everywhere. Late that night, after adjournment, Pillow, Bancroft, and the Polk team prepared to start the ball rolling the next day. Pillow insisted that Polk's nomination must be launched by a northern state and enlisted Bancroft to get that done. At the same time, Pillow lobbied southern states to be ready to switch their support to Polk.

When the eighth roll call began the next morning, New Hampshire became the very first state to record delegate votes for Polk—all six of them—and Massachusetts, Tennessee, Louisiana, and Alabama followed. Now it was a three-man race: Cass, 114 (a drop of 9 votes from the previous ballot); Van Buren, 104 (a gain of 5 votes); and Polk, 44.

As the ninth and final roll call began, Van Buren and Cass backers were angrily accusing one another of buying, badgering, and pressuring delegates to switch votes. In the clash, a Pennsylvania delegate began to extol Polk's virtues as the "bosom friend of Old Hickory . . . a pure, whole hog, Loco Foco Democrat . . . against the Bank of the United States and all corrupting monopolies." [20] Maine jumped from Van Buren to Polk, and the run was on. The Virginia and New York delegates caucused and returned to the floor to endorse Polk. Benjamin Butler, who with Silas Wright led the Van Buren forces, wept as he conceded New York's votes to the Tennessean, describing Polk as "honest, capable, and faithful to the Constitution." [21]

The momentum swept the assembly, and within minutes a hostile crowd was seized by mass euphoria, as one speech after another reminded them of the virtues of this loyal party man from Tennessee. Polk was unanimously acclaimed the nominee. Within minutes, at the urging of Cave Johnson and Gideon Pillow, Silas Wright was nominated by acclamation as the vice presidential candidate. Sharing Butler's sentiments, Wright declined, loyal to the last to Van Buren. The delegates then turned with enthusiasm to Governor George Dallas of Pennsylvania, who gladly accepted second place on the ticket. Comity had been created out of chaos. The Democratic party had a nominee and a platform that included acquiring Texas and the Oregon Territory for the Union.

The Whigs seemed equally pleased. Some laughed at the news about Polk's nomination; others scoffed or cursed. They predicted the demise of the Democratic party under the weak, two-time loser for governor of the party's home state. The *Globe*, the Democratic party booster, reported that Clay, on receiving word, erupted, "Beat again by hell."[22] The race was on.

THE POLITICS OF SLAVERY

Clay and Polk, hoping to be national candidates, came to the campaign as slaveholders from adjoining southwestern states. Polk had the popular side of the Texas annexation issue, but the Tennessean could not afford to be tainted with John C. Calhoun's insistence that Texas come into the Union as a slave state. Polk's position was that if and when annexation came, Texans would decide the question. This was hardly the high moral ground, but it was safe political ground in the North and in the South. Historians generally agree that presidential aspirants such as Polk, Clay, Jackson, Van Buren, and Buchanan had no option but to tolerate the institution of slavery. To stand openly for abolition was to invite defeat at the polls, gamble with dismemberment of the Union, and risk civil war.

Polk was acculturated by a lifelong reliance on slave labor in a racist agrarian society. Reared in a family that owned slaves, he accepted indentured servitude as a way of life. When his father moved the family over the mountains to Tennessee, slaves helped make the journey bearable, then helped clear the land and construct the homes where they lived. Slaves tilled the fields to raise the crops that fed them. At the time of his son's marriage to Sarah,

Sam Polk gave the couple a slave boy, Elias, as a wedding present. When Sam died, he owned forty slaves, two of whom came to Polk. In order to make prosperous his farm properties in western Tennessee and Mississippi, Polk bought and bartered slaves throughout his political career, including his presidency. He needed them, leaned on them, profited from their uncompensated labor, and even hired them out, pocketing the income from their sweat.

While he said he opposed separating slave parents from their children, he sometimes permitted it. He fired plantation overseers when he learned that they abused his slaves, but somehow did not consider beating them to be abusive. In 1830, when a bill was introduced in Congress to ban the lash as a method of punishment, he voted against it. "A slave," he philosophized, "dreads the punishment of stripes more than he does imprisonment." Whippings, he felt, also had "a beneficial effect upon his fellow-slaves."[23]

At the same time, he comprehended the core injustice of the system. In his very first speech on the floor of Congress, he called slavery "a common evil," a "peculiar delicacy," and an "unfortunate subject." He acknowledged that Africans in bonds were "rational," and that they were "human beings."[24] But not once did he make any effort, in Congress or in the presidency, to cure the common evil or to decry the fact that rational human beings were held in chains, beaten, and sold, like cattle or land, for cash and credit. Never did he utter a word of leadership to condemn the inhumanity of the institution.

Robert Remini wrote of Jackson, "He was a racist (not that he had the faintest idea what that meant)." So was Polk—and, as Remini added, so were "most Americans at the time."[25]

Not all, by any means. The abolitionist movement had its strongest support in the North, but in every state, including Tennessee and Kentucky, there were voters who deplored the hypocrisy of a nation, rhetorically committed to liberty, that routinely enslaved African Americans. To abolitionists, the phrase "all men are created equal" meant *all*. At the same time, the nullifiers were poised to lead their southern states out of the Union should slavery be abolished. Polk's campaign challenge would be to carefully chart a course that promoted his stand on Texas but steered away from any slavery controversy.

Throughout his political career he had declined to become embroiled emotionally as the abolitionists argued the imperative of human liberty while the nullifiers argued the imperative of agrarian prosperity. As a member of Congress, he had called the conflict between the two sides "amusing to witness. . . . An opposition man from the North presents a petition [favoring abolition], whereupon a Nullifier from the South . . . springs upon it and makes an inflammatory speech. . . . The game is well understood here."[26]

When he became Speaker, it was neither "amusing" nor "a game." A series of abolitionist petitions infuriated nullifiers, and Representative John Hammond of South Carolina branded the petitioners "ignorant fanatics,"[27] touching off a debate that was difficult for Polk to manage. It raged for weeks. When a majority of the House, weary of the hostility, voted to impose a gag rule on all future antislavery petitions, Polk was delighted. He once had declared that slavery was "evil." Never as House Speaker or chief magistrate would he repeat that declaration. And as a presidential candidate he would stay as far away as possible from the issue.

"FAIR AND JUST PROTECTION"

If Texas and slavery were two potentially hot issues in the contest of 1844, the tariff—taxes on foreign imported goods—was a scalding third. In the industrial North, high tariffs on imports were favored because they protected American manufacturing, the lifeblood of that region's economy. In the agrarian South, high tariffs were deplored because they imposed higher consumer prices on a region that relied so heavily on a cotton economy and had to buy high-priced consumer goods that were taxed.

In 1828, Congress passed, and President Adams signed, a bill
with duties so punitive that southern leaders called it "the Tariff of
Abominations."[28] It was the tariff, and not slavery, that had led an
irate Calhoun to develop the theory of nullification, insisting that
any state government that disapproved of a punitive federal act
had the constitutional right to secede from the Union. As a member of Congress, Polk had won a reputation as a low-tariff man,
consistently voting to protect the region that elected him. Tariffs
that protected the North, he felt, imposed a baseline economic
injustice—another means of favoring the rich to the detriment of
the working middle class and poor of the South.

Clay's record of favoring tariffs was longer than Polk's stand
against them. While Calhoun growled in pain from the punitive
Tariff of Abominations, Clay, as Adams's secretary of state, cele-
brated it, anticipating what a federal tariff surplus would do to
promote internal improvements. Now, for both Polk and Clay, the
tariff was a double-edged sword that cut one way in the South and
the other in the North.

As the Democrats' elation following Polk's nomination receded
in the hours after the convention, his past stands on issues began
to be viewed carefully—especially his low-tariff votes in Congress,
which now came under close scrutiny from northern members of
his party. Pennsylvania, a state suffering from economic distress,
relied heavily on protective tariffs and had benefited from the Tariff
of Abominations. The state's leaders, along with those in New York
and New Jersey, felt jerked around by tariff bills that first raised,
then lowered rates. They immediately turned to their outgoing governor, George Dallas, now Polk's vice presidential running mate, for
an answer on what to expect from Polk.

On the morning after the nomination, Robert Walker, the Mississippi senator who would become a valuable economic adviser
as secretary of the Treasury, wrote Polk from Baltimore, "There is
but one question which can by any possibility defeat your election. It is the tariff." His own low-tariff sentiments concurred with

Polk's, but he added, "I represent one state; you are to be the representative of the democracy of the union." He recommended that Polk "go first for such a tariff as will supply the wants of the Government economically administered; second, . . . within this range . . . go for such just and fair measures as will embrace all the great interests of the whole union and as will . . . afford equal and adequate protection to American industry in all its branches."[29]

Jack Donelson, after consulting with Dallas, suggested to the candidate, "[Say] in the main that you agreed with General Jackson as was proved by your cordial and public support of his administration."[30] That was a crutch that would not get Polk far down the campaign trail.

Cave Johnson had heard from New York, Pennsylvania, and Louisiana Democrats "deeply interested" in Polk's position on the tariff and wrote to Polk, "I need not remind you of the importance of not saying too much."[31] The next day Cave offered another crutch: "The President has nothing to do with the tariff except sign the bill."[32] Polk's friends knew that his problem was his earlier antitariff statements. In 1829, while running for reelection to Congress, he had said that "it must ever be unjust to tax the labor of one class of society to support and fatten another."[33] He had spoken and voted that way consistently in the House. Never had he been challenged on this position until he won the nomination.

In a letter to Polk, John Slidell, a Louisiana congressman, worried about the duties on sugar. In Pennsylvania, Isaac McKinley, editor of the *Harrisburg Democratic Union*, wrote, "All we ask . . . is a revenue tariff . . . adjusted as to afford protection to our iron and coal." Congressman John Kane of Philadelphia joined the chorus and suggested a position of "dignified reserve" (which meant "don't attack high tariffs").[34]

Three weeks after the convention, Senator Walker and Congressman Charles J. Ingersoll of Pennsylvania collaborated on a letter to Polk, warning, "You cannot remain silent without defeating the ticket. . . . The friends of Mr. Clay are so very sanguine of success in Pennsylvania. . . . The tariff [issue] is much stronger now throughout the Union than it ever was before."[35]

Polk carefully crafted a letter to Congressman Kane creatively designed to try to appease both the North and South simultaneously. "I am in favor of a tariff for revenue, such as one that will yield a sufficient amount to the Treasury to defray expenses of the Government, economically administered," he wrote. Following Robert Walker's advice, he added that he also supported duties that would give "reasonable incidental protection to our home industry. . . . It is the duty of the Government, to extend as far it may be practicable to do so, by its revenue laws . . . fair and just protection to all the great interests of the whole Union."[36] Those were the words northern Democrats were waiting for. The Kane letter was widely circulated in the newspapers of Pennsylvania and New York. Gideon Pillow, fearful that the position would lose southern votes, wrote hurriedly to try to stop its circulation, but he was too late. Northern Democrats spread the word that they could count on Polk for a protective tariff. That isn't what he said—but it was what he wanted them to believe. Southern Democrats knew that the thrust of the statement was benign when compared with where Clay stood on the same issue. The nullifiers were upset with the concession to the North, but Calhoun, ambitious to stay on as Polk's secretary of state, kept his minions quiet. The Whigs, knowing doublespeak when they heard it, were apoplectic.

THE DARK HORSE CAMPAIGN

A presidential race in the first half of the nineteenth century was quite different from anything twenty-first-century voters would recognize. First, a candidate for the highest office was expected to become more withdrawn than active. The solicitation of votes was thought unseemly for the most exalted post in government. Propriety aside, from a practical point of view, campaigning far and wide would effectively break off contact between the candidate and his managers in several states. The slowness and uncertainty of travel and communication made it necessary for the nominee to remain in one place, where he could provide his supporters with letters, statements, ideas, responses to charges, and answers to questions. While getting the news from Nashville to New York could take days, the process would be further delayed if the candidate was on the road and unreachable.

The Whigs were infatuated with their successful "Log Cabin and Hard Cider" campaign of 1840, which was filled with hype and hustle, sloganeering, colorful lyrics, and catchy jingles. Both sides would try to replicate that this year, but it all seemed to ring like a cracked bell. The jingles promoting both Clay and Polk strained rhythm, rhyme, and logic:

This lyric, sung to the tune of "Yankee Doodle," was chorused at Polk rallies:

> The Democrats will be triumphant;
> The ladies their charms will display
> And no man will they marry
> Who will vote for Old Henry Clay.[37]

And the Whigs' response:

> Hurrah for Henry Clay,
> Nobody care for Tyler
> Van Buren's out of the way
> And Polk will soon burst his boiler.[38]

It is likely that the Whigs believed that Clay's charm, compared to Polk's prudish personality, gave them an enormous edge. They were campaigning against a humorless, straitlaced little prig from Tennessee. He was, they thought, a fit subject for ridicule. The Whigs launched their campaign playing to what they thought was that weakness, asking the scoffing question, "Who Is James K. Polk?"[39] There was a mocking ring to it, as if Clay, his voice dripping with sarcasm, had coined it himself. It became the Whig mantra shouted out in speeches, published in the Clay partisan press, and laughed at by the party faithful whenever it was heard or read.

It was not as if the nation had never heard of Polk. He had been a controversial congressman and Speaker of the House, praised by friends as Jackson's right arm and condemned by enemies as the old man's tool, a puppet. The Democratic strategists came up with their answer to the question of who Polk was: "Young Hickory!"[40] That nickname created exactly the image they wanted to convey: a strong, new breed of politician who remained true to enduring Jeffersonian values. With Clay as the opponent and Jackson aging and ill, Polk conjured up nostalgic memories of two decades earlier when Old Hickory lost as a result of Clay's "corrupt bargain." And Clay again was the opposition.

Sloganeering was not part of Polk's worries. To turn his nomination into election would require fence mending and bridge building. Van Buren, Cass, Buchanan, Benton, Calhoun, among others, all considered themselves more worthy of the honor, and they represented his party in New York, Michigan, Pennsylvania, Missouri, and South Carolina. He had to win those states to be president. All of those powerful personalities were now contemplating whether to wade in and work to elect Young Hickory—or simply to give his candidacy vaporous lip service, let him lose a respectable race, and try themselves to beat President Clay in four years.

The candidate's first major decision was crucial: to declare for a one-term presidency and convince them all that he meant it.

The stratagem was encouraged by both Jackson and Cave Johnson. On June 12, six weeks after he was nominated, he announced that if elected, he would "enter upon the discharge of the high and solemn duties, with the settled purpose of not being a candidate for reelection."[41] It was a pledge he would keep. Next, without promising anything, he had to hold out the possibility to all of them that his administration would rely on them, perhaps as cabinet officers, or foreign ministers, or close advisers, to help him run the government. Since he was the youngest among all of these vain titans—and would be the nation's youngest president—it was not difficult to let them think he might need them.

Van Buren was a special problem. His pride was hurt. He felt his party had robbed him. He would want no cabinet position for himself but would expect Polk to offer the top cabinet job, secretary of state, to Silas Wright, Benjamin Butler, or some other of his intimate associates. Calhoun, already Tyler's secretary of state, certainly would hope to stay in that post and complete the annexation of Texas. Polk would let him dream. It would not be long before Duff Green, who always carried mail for Calhoun, wrote a letter urging that Polk keep the Great Nullifier in the top cabinet post as a bow to the South. Young Hickory after his election would disappoint both Calhoun and Van Buren, but for the course of the campaign all doors were kept open and every ambition oiled.

Then there was President Tyler. Nominated at his own splinter party convocation and living with a new bride and a painful sense of rejection, he was acting very much like a spiteful candidate. He was hardly a stupid man, and he knew he had no chance with the country so sharply divided along hard party lines. But he craved respect and was hurt by snide criticisms in both Whig and Democratic newspapers. Had Van Buren been the Democratic nominee, Tyler might have had some chance as the only pro-Texas candidate in the race. With Polk's strong position favoring annexation, Tyler knew he was out of it. He would be looking for a graceful exit with praise, not criticism, for moving forward on Texas. Polk was more than willing for him to get it—and to get him out of the race.

Tyler was particularly irritated by a series of journalistic needles from Francis Blair of the *Globe*. Polk urged Old Hickory to write

Blair and ask him not to further antagonize Tyler. Jackson's directive
to the *Globe* editor was pointed: "Support the cause of Polk and
Dallas and let Tiler [*sic*] alone."[42] Strangely, Blair was sticking barbs
in Polk as well as Tyler. "None can fail to have observed the coldness
or indifference of the Globe," Polk wrote to Jack Donelson.[43]

Jackson then drafted a masterful letter to his former White
House resident guest William B. Lewis, still working as an official
of the Treasury Department, and directed Lewis to take it to Tyler.
In it he expressed his high personal regard for the president but
added that in his considered view Tyler, as a third-party candidate,
could not be elected. Old Hickory then put it straight to Tyler. If
he did not withdraw as a candidate, he would be "charged with
conniving with Clay and the Whigs," who had expelled him from
the party. It was a friendly letter, with a sharp edge. Tyler, said
Jackson, deserved to leave office with praise and "much credit" for
his patriotic leadership of the country during a difficult time.[44]

This letter, typically respectful and friendly, made the difference. Tyler later said it convinced him to get out of the race. When
he withdrew, Jackson, pleased with himself, predicted in a burst of
overoptimism that Polk would carry twenty-two states. (He carried only fifteen.)

Polk understood the power of Jackson's pen and kept him busy.
At one point during the race, Sam Houston, frustrated by U.S.
inaction on annexation, let it be known that he was flirting with
the idea of signing treaties with Britain and France as protectors
against a Mexican invasion. Jackson sent him "as strong a letter
as [he] could dictate," warning the Texas president against any
alliance with European governments.[45]

Mudslinging inevitably came to the campaign, aimed at both
Polk and Clay. The Whigs had a tough time nailing Polk with the
sort of personal dirt that was editorial grist for every presidential
election mill. He had led an exemplary married life and was never
known to carouse or gamble. He drank in moderation and could
only have been accused, as Houston once said, of an addiction to

water. He showed up at church with Sarah too often to be attacked as an unbaptized non-Christian. In Ohio, Democrats came together to pass a resolution juxtaposing Polk's reputation with Clay's: the Tennessean, they said, was "distinguished for all the moral attributes which adorn the private man and make a good citizen"; the Kentuckian, on the other hand, was "notorious for his fiendish and vindictive spirit, for his disregard of the most important moral obligations, for his blasphemy, his gambling propensities, and for his frequent and blood-thirsty attempts upon the lives of his fellow-man."[46] With some ten weeks left in the campaign Clay wrote to his friend John Clayton, "I believe I have been charged with every crime enumerated in the Decalogue."[47] Indeed he had. The most appalling document the Democrats produced recited just how he had offended the Ten Commandments: blaspheming, gambling, and engaging in debaucheries "too disgusting to appear in public print."[48]

Whigs searched the Polk family tree for a flaw and came up with a charge that his grandfather Ezekiel had been a Tory sympathizer during the Revolutionary War. The criticism of Ezekiel had originated four years earlier in an eastern Tennessee newspaper and now was picked up by Whig editors and stump speakers across the South. Polk resented any suggestion that cowardice ran in the family and from June until September became absorbed with the subject as he wrote and received more than thirty letters dealing with it. He required an enormous commitment of research, travel, and energy from his Knoxville friend Dr. J. M. G. Ramsey, a historian, to get the vindication of Ezekiel published in circular form. Polk insisted that ten thousand copies of it be distributed and that Democratic newspapers publish it.

The facts were that Ezekiel, eccentric and bullheaded all his life ("Is he not a strange old man?" his son Sam once remarked), had taken "protection" from British troops when General Charles Cornwallis occupied North Carolina in 1780.[49] In order to protect his land from confiscation, he had promised not to act in a

hostile way toward the invaders. Later, he had served in battles against the British, and, in 1782, the year after the war ended, he was elected sheriff, an indication of the esteem in which he was held by his fellow citizen-patriots. Ramsey urged Polk to ignore the charges because, as he wrote on July 10, "admitting that E. P. had taken protection . . . would be trumpeted forth that we had admitted all that was charged."[50] Polk paid no heed. Names of people who had known Ezekiel were collected and testimonials and affidavits solicited extolling his grandfather's patriotism. This was vintage Polk obsessiveness. His family's good name was under attack, and no issue was as important to him until it was answered to his personal satisfaction.

A far more serious charge, invented from the whole cloth, was an article published in the *Ithaca (N.Y.) Chronicle* claiming that Polk branded his initials on the shoulders of forty of his slaves. The "common evil" was to be injected into the campaign after all. The news story became known as the *Roorbach Fraud*.[51] The newspaper claimed that it was reprinting an extract from something called *Roorbach's Tour Through the Western and Southern States in 1836*, by one Baron Roorbach. It turned out that the book itself was fictional—a sort of invented vapid version of Tocqueville's classic—and that the segment mentioning the branded slaves was lifted from yet another book, by G. W. Featherstonhaugh, that never mentioned Polk's name. The newspaper article, signed by "an Abolitionist," was picked up by other papers, but when the fraud was discovered, Democrats screamed so loudly that the *Chronicle* retracted it and papers favorable to Polk exposed the fiction.

"The 'Roorbach' forgery and falsehood is the grossest and basest I have ever known," Polk said. "An infamous falsehood."[52] As it turned out, since Clay relied on slaves to keep Ashland going, and Polk did the same on his plantations in Mississippi and Tennessee, the issue of ownership was rendered virtually irrelevant. Both candidates had gone on record identifying the "peculiar institution" as evil, and neither of them showed any inclination to end

it. If anything, Polk may have gained and Clay suffered because the Whigs were blamed, especially in New York, for the Roorbach forgery.

IT'S POLK AS PRESIDENT

It was a close election in November, a cliff-hanger, as the nominating convention had been, but with far more at stake. As much as anything else, the uniquely dissimilar personalities of the two candidates, their different approaches to political issues, and their contrasting styles combined to influence the result.

Clay lost the election as much as Polk won it. The Great Compromiser approached the race with a wrongheaded sense that he simply was the superior candidate—more astute, more clever, more eloquent, more highly regarded, and demonstrably better equipped to hold the office. It was a dangerous attitude, certain to breed overconfidence, recklessness, and arrogance. At the end of his career, somehow he had convinced himself that he could talk his way out of any thorny problem and never get scratched. His stand against Texas annexation had damaged his prospects badly in the South, so he decided to straighten it out with a letter to an Alabama editor that included this startling assertion: "Personally, I could have no objection to the annexation of Texas." Had he turned around on the issue? Told that he had created confusion, he wrote a second Alabama letter in which he recalled that as secretary of state he had sought to acquire Texas but found that it would likely result in "national dishonor, foreign war and . . . division at home."[53] What he apparently had intended to say in the first letter was that he would have no objection to taking in Texas—if it did not mean dishonor, war, or division. So where was he? His closest advisers couldn't tell.

On slavery, Whigs in the North tried to make Clay out to be an abolitionist, but the ruse didn't work since he was well known as a slave owner. In his second Alabama letter he delivered a brief, disjointed socioeconomic treatise on why slavery would end "some distant day": The "inevitable laws of population" would bring this about when the country became "overwhelmingly populated with white citizens." The enormous supply of white workers would cause the price of labor to drop dramatically and become cheaper than slave labor. His conclusion was that slave labor no longer would be needed. Thurlow Weed, the New York editor and skilled political operative, heard that statement and expressed what most Whigs were feeling. "Things look blue," he said.[54]

Polk and Clay were men of the same world. They came from adjoining western states, born to be politicians, afire with ambition and overbearingly self-conscious. Both sincerely loved their country and were committed to public service as a high calling.

At the same time, in personality, style, character, and philosophy they were poles apart—and all of that made a difference in this election. As Robert Remini explained: "Clay talked too much and wrote too many letters, all of which conjured up in the minds of the electorate a man who would say and do anything to win the White House. Many voters believed that in his efforts over the years to compromise opposing positions he had repeatedly and cynically shifted his positions to advance his political ambitions."[55] Still, the outcome was in doubt until the very end.

In 1844, Election "Day" was actually four days, spanning nearly two weeks. It started on November 1, when Ohio and Pennsylvania kicked off the process, and ended on the twelfth in Vermont and Delaware. All other states cast their ballots on the fourth, except New York, which voted on the fifth. From Columbia, Polk and Sarah waited for news from each state as returns came to them by mail. He lost Vermont and Delaware, the final states to report in, but by that time he had heard from New York and knew that the Regency, Van Buren's informal organization of power brokers, had delivered their state. He was the president-elect. More than two and a half million men cast their ballots, and Polk won by a mere 38,000, a narrow 1.4 percent. He carried fifteen states to Clay's eleven, and his electoral margin was 170 to 105. Had New York, with 36 electoral votes, gone the other way, Clay would have been victorious with 141 votes to Polk's 134. The work of the old Regency veterans, then, with Van Buren providing pained support along with Silas Wright, Ben Butler, and Azariah Flagg, was decisive in electing Polk. While some historians suggest that single-issue abolitionists who voted for James G. Birney, the Liberty party candidate, robbed Clay of victory, that analysis assumes that had Birney not run, the passionate ideologues who voted for him would have flocked in overwhelming numbers to Clay. There is no reason to believe that Birney's abolitionist supporters would have rushed to elect Clay, a man who traded in slaves and was relying on "the inevitable laws of population" to end the evil.[56]

For Polk, the victory toast was sweet, tinged only by a trace of bitters over the loss of his home state by a scant 113 votes. Calhoun's Democratic nullifiers in eastern Tennessee once again stayed away from the polls, and it cost Young Hickory. He was disappointed as much for Jackson as for himself, but the old man, on hearing the result, exulted, "I thank my god that the Republic is safe and that he permitted me to live to see it and rejoice."[57]

In the White House, President Tyler felt he had lost an old enemy. Clay had harassed and harangued him, cast him from the Whig party, and sought to have him impeached. Never would Henry Clay again cause him unease. "He is dead," the president said, "let him rest."[58]

THE TEXAS ANSWER

Before Polk and Sarah left Columbia for the long, joyful journey to Washington, he sent word ahead to Aaron Brown to act as his agent in letting both Democratic and Whig politicians know that he strongly favored immediate action on a Texas annexation resolution in Congress and hoped that initial step would be taken before he was sworn in on March 4. That was good news to President

Tyler and Secretary of State Calhoun, already moving ahead with another proposed congressional resolution favoring annexation. They both wanted to be able to claim credit for the new state—but before the matter was resolved, they would need behind-the-scenes action by Polk to get it done.

On January 25, 1845, with Polk and Sarah still in Columbia, Brown reported on House action: "Our annexation resolutions passed this evening by a majority of 22. . . . Nothing but Texas has engrossed all minds."[59]

In the Senate there still was trouble as two gargantuan egos clashed over the fine print. Thomas Hart Benton, perhaps eager to put his own imprimatur on the momentous acquisition, proposed a Senate resolution, different from the House version. It called for a presidential commission to negotiate final details of the treaty with Texas. Calhoun wailed that the Missourian was grandstanding to take credit away from his great achievement.

By the time Polk arrived in the capital, it was clear that Benton's resolution had stymied Texas annexation, and the president-elect immediately began to maneuver to dislodge and pass the resolution. Senator Willie Mangum of North Carolina reported that Polk "is for Texas, Texas, Texas; and talks of but little else."[60] He, in fact, talked of nothing else to those supporting the contending resolutions. It appears that he led both sides to think he agreed with them, then once in office, delayed for months naming the commissioners Benton's proposal required, while the administration's negotiations with Sam Houston went forward. On December 9, after nine months in office, he notified Congress that the terms of admission to the Union had been reached with Texas, and four days after Christmas Texas became the twenty-eighth state.*

Three years later Polk's duplicity in handling the two resolutions was publicly criticized in separate letters, published in the

---

*Florida had become the twenty-seventh state, admitted on the last day of Tyler's presidency.

New York Post, by Francis Blair and former Ohio senator Benjamin Tappan. Polk, they charged, had double-crossed the Senate by refusing to appoint Benton's commission. In a long, rambling diary entry on July 31, 1848, Polk self-righteously damned his accusers: "The conduct of both [Blair and Tappan] is highly disreputable and dishonorable." He denied that he had deceived the Senate, but Sellers concluded, "Clearly Polk deceived."[61] It was not the first time, nor would it be the last. From his perspective, the end— Texas—justified the means. He chose not to respond publicly to Blair and Tappan. He had won the war to get Texas and had no desire to fight a newspaper battle over how he did it.

5

Measures of a Great President

For forty years, George Bancroft, the gifted historian who served as Polk's secretary of the navy, would remember that moment early in the new administration when Polk, with uncharacteristic animation, shared with him four specific goals that would make his presidency meaningful and memorable. These achievements, Polk believed, would address the immediate and long-term economic and expansionist needs of the nation. They would combine substance and symbolism; pragmatism and vision. These, he told Bancroft, would be his "great measures":[1]

- *He would lower the tariff.* It would set the tone of his administration and send the message to the nation's working agrarian middle class that this was their administration, not subservient to the powerful eastern industrialists.
- *He would re-create Van Buren's independent treasury.* It would bring an end to the financial control of the nation's funds in private banks. The government would secure the people's money. He preferred to call it a "Constitutional Treasury Act," perhaps to put his own new imprint on an old idea and perhaps hoping the name change would make enactment more digestible to Whigs.
- *He would acquire Oregon from the British.* The time had come. The westward expansion demanded it. He would have to make a

strong, direct demand that the British end their shared control of the territory. It would be land governed solely by the United States. He was prepared to draw a line in the great Northwest and deny Great Britain any right to rule the lives of U.S. citizens. He would make "Manifest Destiny" more than a catchphrase for the national dream. He would make it a mandate.

• *He would acquire California from Mexico.* This was to be a continental nation, stretching from ocean to ocean. Mexico would not give up the territory for a song. He would have to pay a dear price for it, but it would be worth it. He would end forever the danger of European intrigues and meddling in the country's domestic affairs.

All of this he intended to do in four years. In Bancroft's mind, there was no wishful fantasizing here. Polk understood the limits of power, the hostility of the Whigs, the dissension and jealousy in his own party, and the intransigence of Great Britain and Mexico. Still, Polk believed he would do it all. A little more than a century later, Harry Truman published his list of eight great presidents and listed Polk, chronologically, behind Washington, Jefferson, and Jackson. "A great president," said the thirty-third chief magistrate of the eleventh. "He said exactly what he was going to do and he did it."[2]

For four years there would be no rest for James Knox Polk. He was an obsessed workaholic, a perfectionist, a micromanager, whose commitment to what he saw as his responsibility led him to virtually incarcerate himself in the White House for the full tenure of his presidency. He rarely went out to visit. Sometimes he took a walk, usually to attend church with his wife. On very rare occasions he took a horseback ride for exercise. He almost never attended a social function and took vacations only when Sarah convinced him that his health demanded it.

At forty-nine, the youngest president was operating in a world he knew well, surrounded by veteran power brokers of his own party: Calhoun, Benton, Cass, Woodbury, and Buchanan. They were men with enormous egos and matching ambitions. Not one of them had lost the fire in the belly, nor surrendered his own dream that one day he would occupy the exalted position that had come to Polk. The new president had made no promises or deals. In his mind, his only real debt was to Andrew Jackson—and he owed him everything. With all of this in mind, he told Cave Johnson: "I intend to be *myself* president."[3]

REBUILDING JACKSONIAN DEMOCRACY

Some ten days after he knew he had won, Polk traveled with Aaron Brown, Tennessee's governor-elect, from Nashville to the Hermitage for a discussion with Jackson about naming his cabinet and plotting the success of the administration. They talked about the need for a harmonious cabinet—six able, knowledgeable politicians who together would help Polk lead the administration, true to the principles of the Jacksonian Democracy. Loyalty would be the first requisite. Names, no doubt, were mentioned, but no decisions were reached and Polk left without making any commitments. Of one thing he was certain. He would not make the mistakes that had led to the cabinet debacle in Old Hickory's administration.

As to personalities, Calhoun, as Tyler's secretary of state, was a special problem. He had launched the initiative on Texas for the Tyler administration and wanted to remain to finish that job, but he carried too much nullification baggage. He would have to go. The president-elect would not have admitted it, perhaps not even to himself, but he was going to be his own secretary of state. He was focusing already on the difficult and delicate business of acquiring California from Mexico and Oregon from Britain. He would want someone overseeing the State Department who was the antithesis of Calhoun; someone Polk could control.

There were natural questions on the mind of the president-elect as he approached the task of cabinet making. Should he wipe out the entire Tyler crew of advisers? Francis Blair was demanding in his *Washington Globe* that the new president clean house. The other option was to select a cabinet whose members included one or more possible successors, so that Polk could have in place a trusted candidate to succeed himself at the end of his term. Jefferson and Jackson, his ideological role models, both had done just that. Jackson now advised Polk, "Keep from your cabinet all aspirants to the presidency."[4] Perhaps Old Hickory realized that his own knighting of Van Buren had caused deep and enduring schisms in the Democratic party. Polk accepted the advice and required from his cabinet officers a pledge that they would not campaign for any office while in the administration.

When the time came to let Calhoun know that he would not remain as secretary of state, Polk personally delivered the bad news. He wanted a completely new cabinet, he said, and offered the nullifier the post of minister to Great Britain. Calhoun said he understood, took the news affably, but declined the offer to go to London. He would soon be back in the Senate, his affability notably less in evidence.

Having told the sitting secretary of state that he would clean out Tyler's cabinet, Polk promptly reneged and appointed his old classmate John Y. Mason, Tyler's secretary of the navy, as his attorney general.

He selected Cave Johnson, his closest friend, as postmaster general and George Bancroft, who had made such a difference in the convention, as secretary of the navy. Robert Walker, the Mississippi senator who had been so helpful in guiding him through the drafting of the ambiguous tariff statement during the campaign, was to be secretary of the Treasury.

Here were four men he knew to be able. They were respected leaders of his party, and their loyalty to him was beyond question.

Skilled in politics and committed to the success of his administration, they would bring a wide range of expertise to the cabinet table. From these men he could expect honest, informed opinion and straightforward advice in a collegial atmosphere. Among them there would be no chance of the tension and anger that pervaded the Jackson cabinet.

Only one of the four, Bancroft of Massachusetts, brought geographic diversity to the inchoate cabinet, and Polk relied on his choices for the State and War Departments to provide a balance that would show his administration to be truly "national." Both selections would cause him trouble.

New York, the state that was widely credited with giving Polk the presidency, was expected to provide the man for the top cabinet job, secretary of state. Van Buren anticipated that he would be asked by Polk to recommend one of his New York allies, Silas Wright or Benjamin Butler, for that assignment. Having lost the nomination to Polk at Baltimore, the former president could have gone back to New York and sulked in defeat. Instead, he rallied his friends to help deliver his home state's crucial electoral votes to the Tennessean. As a result, he felt entitled to recommend the person to head the State Department.

The new president had other ideas. He knew Van Buren's New York associates. They were tough-minded, strong-willed, and remained extremely close to Van Buren. Polk wanted a secretary of state whom he could guide and control. He would not seek him in New York.

Acknowledging at least some debt to the former president, he requested that Van Buren recommend names for secretary of war, rather than secretary of state. Disappointed, the former president accepted the invitation and began to consult with Wright, New York's newly elected governor, who told Van Buren he was not interested in returning to Washington in any role in the Polk administration. Van Buren gave the president's request long and studied consideration (too long and studied, as it turned out), and finally wrote a letter promoting Benjamin Butler or Churchill Cambreleng as war secretary. At the same time, Van Buren warned Polk that there was one New Yorker who, under no circumstances, should get the job: former governor William Marcy. To appoint Marcy to the cabinet would be "a fatal mistake in this state," Van Buren said.[5] The virus of factional politics infected New York as Tennessee, and Marcy had fallen into disfavor with Van Buren. Whether it was impatience or arrogance or both, Polk did not wait for Van Buren's letter of recommendations to arrive at the White House before he named his secretary of war. And he proceeded to make the "fatal mistake." He selected Marcy and later claimed that he was unaware of the friction inside the Democratic party in New York.

It was an unforgettable and unforgivable cut that Van Buren deeply felt. It gave him and his New York Regency colleagues every reason to think Polk an ingrate. The president, for his part, felt no twinge of guilt. He may have suspected that the Van Buren crowd was not really serious about the recommendations of Butler and Cambreleng, since Van Buren's letter was hardly a prompt response to a presidential request. He may have heard that Butler, like Wright, had been less than enthusiastic about returning to Washington to serve in the administration. At any rate, while a measure of cool courtesy defined the ongoing relationship between the president and the former president, the bad feelings persisted. More than two years later, while traveling through New York on a presidential tour, he turned down a chance to visit Van Buren at his home in Kinderhook. The invitation was not sincere, Polk said, and had been extended by the former president only because Van Buren feared "public opinion."[6]

For secretary of state, Polk selected James Buchanan, the Pennsylvania senator who one day would become president. Of all his cabinet appointments, this, the top one, caused Polk the most grief. Vice President George Dallas, himself from Pennsylvania, implored Polk not to give the job to Buchanan. The Democratic party in Pennsylvania, as in New York and Tennessee, was torn by factionalism. If Marcy's appointment was a political slight to Van Buren, Buchanan's designation as secretary of state was a political slap in the face to Dallas. Polk meant it when he said he intended *himself* to be the president, and he disregarded Dallas's plea.

The Buchanan appointment is intriguing because of what Polk certainly knew about the Pennsylvania senator. There had been a bizarre performance by the Pennsylvanian almost twenty years earlier when Buchanan was a newly elected congressman. At the time, preliminary reports of the "corrupt bargain" were circulating in the Washington gossip mill but had not been consummated. Buchanan called on Jackson to propose something close to a corrupt bargain of his own. Jackson was warning his friends that "corruption and sale of public office" were about to take place when Buchanan showed up to confirm Old Hickory's worst fears.[7] Robert Remini described Buchanan's conduct: "He kept winking at Old Hickory as he spoke. . . . Jackson stared in disbelief at the . . . fidgeting little busybody. Everything he had related to . . . his other friends about intrigues and plots now stood twitching before him."[8]

Buchanan led Jackson to believe that Clay's agents had sent him as their messenger, to say that the Kentuckian wanted to be secretary of state. If Jackson would assure Buchanan that Clay would get the post, it could "end the presidential election within the hour." Old Hickory sent him packing. Shortly afterward, when Adams appointed Clay secretary of state, Jackson exposed his strange conversation with Buchanan as proof that he had rejected the corrupt bargain Adams had made. Then, in a gasp of humiliation, the Pennsylvania congressman explained that he had not acted as Clay's intermediary but on his own initiative. Jackson concluded that Buchanan was either a charlatan or a liar.

After that odd incident Buchanan went on to become a power in Pennsylvania politics, and Polk knew that he had worked hard to deliver his state to Jackson in 1828. Old Hickory forgave

Buchanan that quirky introduction, though he never forgot it. As president, Jackson rewarded Buchanan with a two-year ministerial post in Russia but later said, "It was as far as I could send him out of my sight. . . . I would have sent him to the North Pole if we had kept a minister there!"[9]

Buchanan never had married, and there were mean and vicious rumors linking him romantically with Senator William Rufus King of Alabama, his Washington roommate for years. Polk certainly had picked up some of the dirt about them, since his friend Aaron Brown helped spread it. In January 1844, while still a congressman, Brown wrote a "confidential" letter to Sarah Polk, intended as a satirical put-down of King, identifying him as Buchanan's "wife." At the time, King was being touted by Buchanan as Van Buren's potential vice presidential candidate in competition with Polk. Brown apparently was seeking to reassure Sarah that King's campaign was headed downhill and that her husband was more highly thought of. He wrote:

> Mr. Buchanan looks gloomy and dissatisfied and so did his better half . . . by getting a divorce she might set up again in the world to some tolerable advantage. . . . Aunt Nancy may now be seen every day, triged out in her best clothes and smirking about. . . . Gen. [Romulus] Saunders . . . in the presence of Mr. Buchanan and his wife and some others advanced the opinion that neither Mr. Calhoun nor Mr. Van Buren had any chance to be elected [president] and being asked by someone, "who then can be," he forgot himself and said that Col. Polk could run better than any other man in the nation. This of course was highly indecorous toward Mrs. B.[10]

While time and context make the thrust of his letter difficult to follow, there is no doubt that Brown's intent was to label Buchanan and King as lovers. "Aunt Nancy," incidentally, was the name Andrew Jackson had used sometime earlier to refer to King. According to Robert Remini, Henry Clay "rarely missed an opportunity to mock Senator Buchanan" when the two served in the Senate. Remini related an exchange between them in which Clay, "in a softer feminine voice," told Buchanan, "I wish I had a more lady-like manner of expressing myself" and offered to "modulate [his] voice to suit the delicate ear of the Senator."[11]

The gossip was fed by the knowledge that Buchanan had once been betrothed, but the young Philadelphia woman died following an outburst of "hysterics" after the engagement was broken off. Phillip Shriver Klein, Buchanan's biographer, reported that there were suicide rumors and that the attending physician had said, "It is the first instance he knew of hysteria producing death."[12] Her parents would not allow Buchanan to attend the funeral, and his letter of sympathy was returned unopened by her father. Buchanan swore never to marry in honor of her memory. As Michael J. Birkner, one of his biographers, wrote: "Buchanan's love life is inevitably the subject of speculation. What we know would not give even the most adventurous psycho-biographer much to go on."[13]

Birkner described him as a man who had great difficulty making emotional connections with anybody, male or female. The exception to that, Birkner suggested, was "possibly his long-time roommate in Washington, Senator William R. King."[14] (King, incidentally, was elected vice president under Franklin Pierce but died thirty days after he was sworn into office.)

In 1844, when King was sent to France as minister, his farewell letter to Buchanan expresses the hope that his roommate will find no one to replace him in affection. Buchanan's subsequent letter to a woman acquaintance indicates that he did not. "I am now 'solitary and alone,' having no companion in the house with me. I have gone wooing to several gentlemen but have not succeeded with any one of them."[15]

At that time there were numerous members of Congress who shared living quarters, and that may be a logical explanation of the

letter. Whatever Buchanan's sexual preference, times were no more sympathetic to homosexuality in the mid–nineteenth century than in today's world of homophobia. The street was the place for rumors, but the closet was the place for the truth. And whatever the truth, the hurtful conversations among Buchanan's peers must have made life difficult, even for the premier cabinet officer.

Nowhere in his letters or diary does Polk acknowledge any interest or concern about the personal life of his secretary of state. He and Sarah had no secrets, and there can be no doubt that his wife shared with him Aaron Brown's malevolent letter. It made no difference. Buchanan was his choice.

Buchanan, however, was no shrinking violet. He had a burning ambition to be president as well as secretary of state, and though he took strong positions in cabinet meetings, he sometimes shifted stances with the reigning politics. When key issues were brought before the cabinet, his alternating stridency and inconsistency sometimes galled the president, and there would be clashes of will and bad feelings between them.

So the cabinet was formed. The president had put together a group of generalists and asked all of them to express their views on issues, domestic and foreign. He would cross-examine them if he didn't like what he heard. Unlike many presidents, including Jackson, Polk depended on frequent cabinet meetings to keep himself intimately informed on developments in each department. Again, unlike his mentor, there was no kitchen cabinet to second-guess the work of the people he had picked to run the government. He alone did the second-guessing.

POLK STANDS ALONE

Polk's first serious conversations about administration appointments were initiated at the Hermitage with Jackson, but there were limits to the advice he would take, even from Old Hickory,

to whom he owed all. Jackson urged Polk to protect two old Jackson cronies, Francis Blair, the editor of the *Globe*, and William B. Lewis, who had resided at the White House during Old Hickory's years there. Jackson had given Lewis a sinecure as second auditor of the Treasury during his administration, and both Van Buren and Tyler, out of respect for the former president, kept him in that job. Polk, however, never liked or trusted Lewis and ignored Jackson's plea to retain him. He summarily cut him out at the Treasury Department and was unapologetic about it. Jackson, pained, wrote Lewis that he would not "beg" Polk—and that was that.[16]

Blair and his *Globe* had been the Washington press voice of Jackson and Van Buren. Old Hickory tried to sell Polk on the idea that Blair's paper would shield and defend the new administration from attacks in the Whig press, and in return, the *Globe* would continue its lucrative government printing contracts. Polk wouldn't buy it. The *Globe* had been cool to his presidential aspirations well into the campaign, and he thought the editor was condescending to him. The president met with Blair and, as was often the case, dissembled. He led the editor to believe that he would keep him. At that very moment, he had Cave Johnson and Aaron Brown talking to other friendly Democratic editors about replacing Blair. In finally dropping the *Globe* and its editor, the president self-righteously declared, "I will . . . not be controlled by any newspaper."[17] He brought in Thomas Ritchie, the journalist and political leader from Richmond, to become editor of a new administration paper, the *Washington Union*.

"I must be the head of my own administration," Polk said.[18] Jackson, heartsick, growled that it was "loathsome . . . to see an old friend laid aside."[19] Nonetheless, Old Hickory continued to correspond with and support the new president. Two days before Jackson died in June, he wrote Polk his last letter, alerting the president to what he believed was evidence of corruption in the Treasury Department.

THE GOVERNMENT'S PROTECTOR

In his inaugural address President Polk, no longer seeking votes from industrial states, candidly set out his feelings about the tariff. The carefully worded position he had taken during the campaign, in that disingenuous letter to Pennsylvania congressman Kane, had been calculated to lead voters from northern industrial states to believe that he might support some protective tariffs.

Now, elected and never intending to run again, he enunciated his administration's commitment to economic justice as it related to this divisive issue. Any tariff, he said, should be imposed with the chief goal of funding the needs of government. Any protection of industry would be incidental to that need. "To reverse this principle," he said, "would be to inflict manifest injustice upon all other than the protected interests." He ticked off the areas of enterprise composing the nation's industrial base: agriculture, manufacturing, commerce, navigation, and the "mechanic arts." He declared: "To tax one . . . for the benefit of another would be unjust. . . . No one . . . of these interests can rightfully claim an advantage over the others, or be enriched by impoverishing the others. All are equally entitled to the fostering care and protection of the government."[20]

That gave the operative word, *protection,* a different meaning than his Kane letter had conveyed. In levying duties, he now said, "care should be taken . . . not to benefit the wealthy few at the expense of the toiling millions." It was wrong to tax at the lowest rate the "luxuries of life . . . afforded only by the rich." It was equally wrong, he said, to tax at the highest rate "the necessaries of life . . . afforded only by the poor."[21]

Here, in just a few paragraphs, Polk articulated his commitment to a taxing policy rooted in common equity. It drew the line between Democrats and Whigs; between the legacies of Thomas Jefferson and Alexander Hamilton; between Andrew Jackson's philosophy and Henry Clay's. And it defined the fiscal mind-set of the new president.

Secretary of the Treasury Walker, using Polk's inaugural statement as his guide, drafted the low tariff measure that the president sent to Congress. Northern industrialists, forewarned by the inaugural address, "swarmed" into Washington to attempt to defeat Polk's tariff legislation. Their arrival was no surprise to Polk. He knew he would be opposed by "capitalists and monopolists" who had made "enormous profits . . . under the tariff."[22] From the White House he kept track of events at the capital and noted "the most tremendous efforts . . . to defeat the Bill."[23]

His former congressional colleague from Tennessee, Senator Hopkins Turney, warned him that "money would be used, if it could be, to beat the bill." A wealthy manufacturer had approached Turney "two or three times" and tried to bribe him with a loan of "any amount of money he might want." Turney was not for sale. "I was shocked at the story," the president said.[24]

From his first day in office, Polk had complained bitterly about demands made on him by members of Congress to give jobs in government to their constituents or to themselves. At one point he predicted that no future president ever would be reelected to office because of the number of job seekers turned down. Now he moaned that patronage plums he had refused to give senators were costing him support on the tariff bill. As a vote on the measure neared in the Senate, there were threats of Democratic defections. From his days as House Speaker, he was expert at counting heads, and he sensed that if a single Senate backer of his bill flipped against it—or even failed to show up and vote on final passage—the tariff battle would be lost.

Senator Daniel Dickinson of New York, Polk wrote, was among those he feared would defect; the New Yorker's friends at home had not received political appointments. Senator James Semple of Illinois, a constant harpy, was furious because Polk refused him a military generalship. When the president heard that Semple was

packing his trunk to go home, the president rushed the trusted
Cave Johnson, his postmaster general, out into the evening to
catch him. Intercepted at the train depot, the senator showed up
at the White House at eight o'clock at night. Later, in his diary,
Polk recorded Semple's sad story. "He showed me a letter which
he said he had received from Illinois stating that judgments had
been recovered against him in the courts." Semple owed five thousand dollars, and his property was about be taken to satisfy the
notes. There was no claim that enemies of the tariff legislation had
caused Semple's troubles, but for an hour the president made "an
earnest appeal to his patriotism . . . for the sake of the country"[25]
and pleaded with him to stay and vote. Semple reluctantly agreed.

The intense pressure from the lobbyists continued, and Polk
expressed surprise when he learned that his college classmate
Senator William Haywood had resigned and headed home to
North Carolina. "I was astonished," said the president.[26] Perhaps
he was—although not so astonished that he tried to dissuade Haywood. Twice he had invited the North Carolinian to the White
House to try to convince him that lowering the tariff would
enhance the nation's future economic prosperity. At the end of
the second visit, Haywood promised to consider Polk's arguments
until the very moment before he cast his vote. That was not what
the president wanted to hear, and he never counted Haywood as a
supporter of his tariff bill. When his old classmate abruptly quit
and went home, Polk knew the monopolists had lost a vote. Haywood was "an honest and pure man," Polk said. "He was nervous
and had acted hastily."[27]

It finally came down to Tennessee senator Spencer Jarnagin.
Jarnagin told the president he planned to vote "Nay"—against the
bill. Then Aaron Brown, Tennessee's new governor, prodded the
state general assembly to instruct the senator to vote with Polk.
Jarnagin equivocated until the last moment, then voted "Aye." On
July 28, 1846, the bill passed by a 28-to-27 vote, with Vice President Dallas breaking the tie. Had Semple gone home or Haywood

stayed, the bill would have gone down to defeat. Dallas's vote was denounced by fellow Democrats at home in Pennsylvania. The influence of the lobbyists upset Polk, and he later promised that on leaving office he would write a book exposing "the selfish and corrupt considerations which influence . . . public men."[28]

In the 1846 congressional elections, the Democrats lost the House, and Buchanan, irked over Polk's new tariff, told him that the legislation had cost him votes in Pennsylvania. Frederick Merk, the Harvard historian, more accurately pointed to growing discontent and Whig dissent over the war with Mexico. Polk told Buchanan he had no intention of backing away from his victory on the tariff.

The victory lowering the tariff should have welded Senator John C. Calhoun to the Polk administration. It didn't. Nothing Polk could do would gain Calhoun's support. Shortly before Christmas 1845, the old nullifier turned up at the White House for a private conversation. "He appeared to be in fine humour," the president reported in his diary. When the discussion turned to other issues—Texas and Oregon—something in Calhoun's tone convinced Polk "that Mr. Calhoun will be very soon in opposition to my Administration."[29] By April 1847 he had proved himself prophet: "I now entertain a worse opinion of Mr. Calhoun than I have ever done before. He is wholly selfish and . . . has no patriotism. A few years ago he was the author of Nullification and threatened to dissolve the Union on account of the tariff. During my administration the reduction of duties which he desired has been obtained, and he can no longer complain. No sooner is this done than he selected slavery upon which to agitate the country, and blindly mounts that topic as a hobby."[30]

THE FIRST LADY

Sarah Childress Polk possessed all the natural social elegance that her husband lacked. She had charm, wit, and poise. With an intellect that matched his, she made for him an ideal mate and for the nation an ideal first lady. She had the rare capacity to move with a friendly demeanor when she was with his enemies as well as his friends. She had known from the outset that she had married a committed politician. She never could have guessed that he would take her all the way to the pinnacle of political power, but in every way she was up to it, offering advice, support, and humor to a man whose ego sometimes alienated almost everyone else around him.

Often she found subtle ways to tell him that perhaps he should rethink a position. On one occasion when they were traveling, he needed money from their suitcase so that he could pay a bill in metal coinage. She let him know that opposition politicians, who favored paper money, had the best side of that issue.

Twice each week she threw open the doors of the executive residence and welcomed any citizen who wished to visit. It often was an ordeal for him, put upon as he was by people demanding jobs, asking favors, begging handouts, and soliciting for charities. His feigned hospitable manner often was obvious, but Sarah managed beautifully, often handling the welcomes alone when he was occupied with presidential duty.

Her friends among Washington wives comfortably crossed party lines, and always her ear was to the ground and she let him know what was said. She kept abreast of news reports regularly, alerting him to items he might otherwise have missed.

Aware of the religious void in his nonsectarian life, she pushed him to go to church with her as often as she could. She was a popular hostess, allowing wine but no hard liquor served on the presidential premises. Sometimes she sought to restrict the use of the residence on Sunday out of respect for the Sabbath rule.

For as long as they were there, she worked to make thousands of visitors feel at home, but the ultimate test came three years into the Polk presidency when Henry Clay finally came calling at the White House. It was a surprise visit, and Polk, stiff and civil,

apparently handled the greeting in good form. Clay told him he
had not visited earlier because he had not been sure Polk would
want him to come, given their political rivalry. The president
assured him he was completely amenable to his visit and honored
by his presence. It was Sarah, however, who moved in and made
Clay feel right at home.

The needling old chameleon, who could charm a rattlesnake
with compliments, told Sarah that he had heard great things
about her administration of the White House. But, he teased,
there was a difference of opinion from what he had heard about
her husband's performance. She read him perfectly. She was glad
he approved of her performance as first lady, she said, and added:
"if a political opponent of my husband is to succeed him I have
always said I prefer you, Mister Clay, and in that event I will be
most happy to surrender the White House to you." Polk recorded
in his diary that "there was a hearty laugh and he left in excellent
humor."[31]

As gracious as she could be, she sometimes secretly would cut
from the White House invitation list the names of people she
knew the president disliked. John Van Buren, the son of the former president, for example, never made it to a White House din-
ner. Ultimately, the president would discover what she had done
and was amused. Childless, Sarah dedicated herself to the well-
being of her husband—his health, his comfort, his success—and
found great satisfaction in it.

DOCUMENTING A PRESIDENCY

Had he lived a century later, it is not unlikely that Polk, like Presi-
dents Kennedy, Johnson, and Nixon, would have tape-recorded his
White House conversations to make certain that there was pre-
served an accurate record by which history could fairly judge him.
Like Nixon and Johnson, who taped themselves indiscriminately
(Kennedy was far more selective in recording himself), Polk often

told his journal too much, a driven chief magistrate who recorded with tedious fidelity the crises and controversies that confronted him, often at his own hand.

In August 1845, after five months in office, he decided to keep the daily record. Clearly, he did not want the work of his administration misunderstood. It was a time-consuming undertaking, and his commitment to it over three years is impressive.

For all the color and excitement the daily log brings to an understanding of his presidency, Polk, paradoxically, must be read as a brooding and humorless man. He wrote with effortless clarity and opinionated candor that revealed the shadowed side of a conflicted personality. Sometimes he presents himself as demanding to the point of unreasonableness, determined to the point of stubbornness, self-righteous to the point of paranoia. There are moments, as he vents his anger or frustration, when the emotional release almost seems therapeutic. More than anything else, he comes across as intensely partisan, at times blindly so.

Anything that was Whig was suspect, reactionary, wedded to money, probably corrupt, out to embarrass him and defeat his programs. Democrats in Congress, who joined Whigs on votes crucial to the administration's success, were treasonous in Polk's mind. He did not need to make political enemies, he assumed them, accepted their opposition as natural, demonized them, sought to engage and defeat them. The diary was the repository of all these views. The name *Whig*, adopted for the party by Henry Clay, was a negative, synonymous with *Federalist*—the word that from childhood had been close to a vulgarism. In September 1848, he told his diary that he had fired Benjamin Butler, the U.S. attorney in New York, because Butler had "bolted" the Democratic party and "united himself with Federalists and abolitionists."[32]

The diary exposes his deepest aggravations, his anger, his quirks, and his arrogance. When three Democratic senators, Simon Cameron of Pennsylvania, James D. Westcott of Florida, and John

C. Calhoun of South Carolina, joined the Whigs to defeat Polk's appointee as collector of the port of Philadelphia, he told his diary exactly what he thought of them: "[Cameron] is a managing, tricky man in whom no reliance is to be placed. He professes to be a Democrat, but he has his own personal and sinister purposes. . . . I consider him little better than a Whig. Westcott, though elected as a Democrat, I consider a Whig. Of Mr. Calhoun, I forbear to express an opinion, further than to say that his ambition is destroying him."[33]

He had this strange sense of propriety. Some avowed enemy in Congress could walk into the White House, and he would welcome him with the restrained politeness of the father of the bride at a wedding reception. There would be an affable encounter with no hint of animosity. Then, that night upstairs with his diary, he let his good manners fly out the window. Cameron and Westcott crossed him a second time by voting with the Whigs to reject one of his nominees for the Supreme Court. Word shortly reached Polk that the two men gloated over administering the defeat to their president and that Westcott was reported to have said, "The only way to treat an ugly Negro was to give him a d——n drubbing— and he would learn to behave himself."[34] In other words, they had given Polk the damn drubbing and expected him to behave.

Soon afterward, Cameron brought a friend to the White House to meet Polk, who treated the senator with feigned civility. He told the diary what he really thought: Cameron was "hypocritical. . . . I felt great contempt for him."[35]

Three months passed before Westcott showed his face at the presidential residence, and Polk "treated him as the president should treat any citizen in his own mansion."[36] Ninety days had gone by, but he vividly remembered what the senator had said and the allusion to the "drubbing given to me, according to the low and vulgar language of Mr. Westcott. . . . I cannot express my contempt for a Senator who could be capable of such coarseness and vulgarity."[37]

In fact, Polk remembered insults large and small and was unforgiving. Another unwelcome guest was his fellow Tennessean Andrew Johnson, who one day would call the White House home. Johnson heard through the Washington grapevine that he was out of favor with the president, and he visited him to deny emphatically "that he was opposed to [Polk] or [his] administration." The president reported that he courteously heard out Johnson's avowal of loyalty. He then wrote in his diary that Johnson never had been friendly to him, and as evidence he recalled the word the congressman reportedly had uttered when he learned of Polk's presidential nomination at Baltimore. It was *humbug*.[38]

There are flashes of his healthy ego to be found in the pages of his daily log. In September 1848, Polk confided in his diary that he was capable of running the government without the cabinet. "I have not had my full cabinet together in council since the adjournment of Congress," he said in a sudden burst of hauteur. During the past five weeks, he added: "I have conducted the Government without their aid. Indeed, I have become so familiar with the duties and working of the Government, not only in general principles but in minute details, that I find but little difficulty in doing this."[39]

On another occasion he described himself as "the hardest working man in the country."[40] As egotistical as it sounds, it well may have been true. He also recorded frequent blunt confrontations with his secretary of state and logged his feelings of mistrust for Buchanan.

THE TREASURY, INDEPENDENT

Polk worried that his refusal to give patronage favors to members of Congress would cost him the Independent Treasury bill. "The danger now is that the great measures of the Session will be defeated from this cause," he said.[41]

This time he misjudged the opposition in Congress. For all the conflict and uncertainty that had attended the administration's struggle to lower the tariff, the Independent Treasury Act turned out to be surprisingly free from contention. This, one of his four "great measures," a move to forever separate private banks from the government's money, would be another step to provide economic justice. It would drive a final nail in the coffin of the Bank of the United States and the so-called pet banks. With it Polk made a bow toward Martin Van Buren, who, as president, had pushed the idea of an independent Treasury through Congress during his administration. It had suffered an early death during the Tyler administration.

Polk preferred to call his version the Constitutional Treasury Act, but by whatever name, the measure would place the people's money in federal fireproof vaults until government bills were due or payrolls had to be met.

In his first message to Congress, Polk had explained the injustice, impracticality, and danger of corruption that threatened when government deposits were in private hands. It was a powerful argument. Opposition to the measure was tepid by comparison to the tariff bill. The president and his administration apparently had to lobby very little for it. During the time it was pending, Polk scarcely mentioned it in his diary, and there was no celebratory entry marking its passage either in the House on April 2, where it carried by a hefty 122-to-66 margin, or in the Senate, where it passed on June 8 by a narrow 3 votes, 28 to 25. His "Constitutional Treasury" was an idea with strong legs. It survived until 1913, when it was replaced by the Federal Reserve System.

MANIFEST DESTINY

On his first day as president, Polk laid a stated claim on the vast and boundless territory of the great Northwest. "Our title to the country of Oregon is clear and unquestionable," he declared at his inaugural.[42] His subsequent message to Congress called for the federal government to provide protection for the stream of settlers threading their way toward the northern Pacific coast. They had heard the call of "Manifest Destiny"—and clearly the spirit of western expansion moved Polk to action. The Oregon land, by treaty, was all under joint control of the United States and Great Britain. Polk wanted clear and sole title to a lion's share of the area.

In London, the government of Sir Robert Peel read Polk's words and heard American sabers rattling. Some congressional firebrands already were warlike in calling for the British to give up their claims on Oregon all the way north to the fifty-fourth parallel. "Fifty-four forty or fight!" was their slogan.

The Tyler administration had earlier proposed that the British give up all land south of the forty-ninth parallel—roughly at the present border line between Washington State and British Columbia. Britain wanted the demarcation along the Columbia River, which would have moved the U.S. ownership southward to about the present border line between Washington and Oregon states. Had the British prevailed, Washington would have remained in their control.

Polk initially left on the table the Tyler administration's offer to establish the line at the forty-ninth parallel. Buchanan sent word of that to Richard Pakenham, the British minister in Washington, and hoped for the best. Lord Pakenham, without bothering to confer with his superiors in London, flatly and rudely rejected the offer. Polk was angered. He instructed Buchanan to write immediately and withdraw the Tyler administration offer. He would show the Brits. He now would push for a line that would give the United States the greatest possible landmass.

On August 26, 1845, the day Polk launched the diary, the cabinet engaged in what the president called "a very important conversation," but it smacked more of an argument between the secretary of state and the president.

Buchanan told the cabinet, "If the president's views were carried out—demanding land north of the 49th parallel—we would
have a war" with England. Polk shot back, "If we do have war it
will not be our fault." If that meant "fifty-four forty or fight," he
was ready to go to war.

Buchanan flatly told the president that the American people
would not support him in a war over the drawing of a line in the
Northwest. A war, he lectured, should be waged or some higher
ground—for liberty or for honor.

The president warmly disagreed. When the people saw the evidence against the British claim to American soil, he predicted,
"they would be prompt and ready to sustain the Government."

He advised Buchanan to take off the gloves and get tough with
Pakenham. He wanted the British government to understand that
his administration would be demanding more northern territory,
not less. As he often did when he lost an argument with Polk,
Buchanan had a fallback position. In light of the growing stress
between the United States and Mexico, and the threat of an invasion of Texas, why not delay any response to Pakenham until the
Mexican picture was clearer?

Polk was firm: "We should do our duty towards both Mexico
and Great Britain and firmly maintain our rights—and leave the
rest to God and country." Buchanan said cryptically, "God would
not have much to do in justifying us in a war for the country north
of 49°." But he followed instructions and notified the British that
the offer to draw the line at the forty-ninth parallel was withdrawn.[43]

Four days later, Oregon again was the lead item on the cabinet's agenda, and there was yet another bristling exchange
between Polk and Buchanan. The secretary had handed the message on Oregon to the British minister and was not happy. "Well,
the deed is done," he complained pointedly to Polk. "[I] do not
think it was the part of wise statesmanship to deliver such a paper
in the existing state of our relations with Mexico." Polk warmly

disagreed. He was glad it was delivered because "it was right, in itself."[44]

As summer turned to fall, Polk was contemplating war on two fronts as he tried to read mixed messages that emanated from both London and Mexico City. While Pakenham seemed unresponsive, uncooperative, and unfriendly on the Oregon issue, Prime Minister Robert Peel reportedly was less belligerent. South of the border, the Mexican Congress seemed ready to wage war over Texas annexation, but President José Joaquín de Herrera, leading a nation that was financially bankrupt, was reluctant to fight unless his Congress funded the army. As detailed negotiations on annexing Texas went forward with Sam Houston's republic, Polk's cabinet, nervous about Britain and Oregon, advised the president to dispatch Brigadier General Zachary Taylor into the Texas territory in the event Mexico invaded. Polk's "confidential agent" inside Mexico, Dr. William Parrott, a former Virginia dentist, reported that President Herrera might be overthrown by a military coup.[45] That raised two questions: Would the threat of being deposed stiffen Herrera's resolve to make war? Would a new president, should the coup succeed, be more warlike than the incumbent? Either answer suggested that war with Mexico might be unavoidable.

By November, Polk was feeling a bit better about relations with both the British and the Mexicans. He heard from London that Lord Aberdeen, the British foreign minister, favored a pacific approach to the United States and regretted that Pakenham arbitrarily had rejected the Tyler administration proposal. London apparently wanted to negotiate, not fight. Then Dr. Parrott arrived in Washington with even better news. The Mexicans had indicated that they would receive Polk's minister to discuss resolving the issues separating them. The president immediately assigned the post to former congressman John Slidell from Louisiana, who was bilingual and friendly to the administration. He would travel at once and present his credentials to the Mexican government. By the time he reached Mexico City, the mood had shifted again and the good news had soured. The Mexicans gave Slidell short shrift and sent him packing. The overthrow of the Herrera government came, but the new president, General Mariano Paredes y Arrillaga, was more hard-nosed than Herrera had been. War with Mexico was imminent.

As to Oregon, the British at month's end seemed pliable. With Polk still running a bluff for more land, Buchanan came to the cabinet with a report that he had been feeling the pulse of Congress and discovered real opposition to the administration's insistence on trying to take territory above the forty-ninth parallel. Polk was nettled by it. "Your channels of information are very different from mine," he said. "Not one in ten of the members" of Congress opposed taking as much of the northern land as possible.

The secretary again lectured Polk. "Your greatest danger," Buchanan said, "is that you will be attacked for having a warlike tone."

"My greatest danger," the president snorted, "is that I would be attacked for having yielded to what was done by my predecessors."[46]

In late December, Senator John C. Calhoun turned up at the president's office "in a fine humour"[47] with Oregon on his mind. As Tyler's secretary of state and the architect of the administration's offer to put the line at the forty-ninth parallel, he had a personal interest in a peaceful solution. When he departed, Polk, suspicious that he had been talking to Buchanan, guessed that Calhoun's "fine humour" with the administration soon would evaporate. He was right.

"A grave discussion"[48] on the Oregon issue dominated the cabinet meeting two days before Christmas. Pakenham had given no ground, and many in Congress still were ready to fight. The cabinet thought there might be war. The time had come to prepare the nation for it. Polk told one member of Congress, "The only way to treat John Bull is to look him in the eye."[49]

And suddenly, the British blinked. Word arrived from Louis McLane, the U.S. minister to London, that while the Peel government was preparing for war, Lord Aberdeen was asking whether the United States would consider a proposal to set the line at the forty-ninth parallel—the original Tyler administration line. But would the hotheads in Congress accept a treaty for a line below the fifty-fourth parallel? Polk reported in his diary, "In all this Oregon discussion . . . too many Democratic Senators have been more concerned about the presidential election in '48, than they have been about settling Oregon. . . . For the sake of the country I deeply deplore it."[50]

Senator Lewis Cass, the former general from Michigan who would win the Democratic nomination in 1848, was an outspoken hawk, in favor of "54-40." The usually warlike Calhoun, however, now was dovelike. Polk asked the cabinet for a recommendation on whether to send the British offer to the Senate. Every member present voted in favor—except, amazingly, James Buchanan. He completely reversed himself. He was silent until finally Polk pushed him into declaring where he stood. With "the true friends of the administration"—those who favored the fifty-four forty line; Polk was "backing out" on them.[51]

In fact, Buchanan was backing out on Polk. It seemed clear to the president that the secretary of state was letting his ambition for the presidency rule his judgment. It was as if he sought to out-Cass Cass. Other members of the cabinet became testy with Buchanan. Walker pointedly remarked that no "member of the Cabinet should exert an influence" upon the senators on this subject.[52] The British treaty offer was submitted to the Senate, with the secretary of state morose about it. At first he refused Polk's request to help draft the Oregon message to the Senate and patronizingly announced that he might write a paper of his own after Polk drafted his version. Infuriated, the president demanded to know: "Do you wish . . . to draw up a paper on your own in order to make an issue with me?" It stopped Buchanan cold. He knew he had gone too far. He told the president that this remark "struck him through the heart." There was an uncomfortable moment, and the two men backed away from an irrevocable split. Each professed friendship. After what Polk would describe as "a most unpleasant interview," the secretary of state went home.[53]

Within a week the Senate approved the proposal by a vote of 38 to 12. The Oregon Territory—which would ultimately make up all of Washington and Oregon and parts of Wyoming and Idaho—belonged to the United States. Another of Polk's major goals had been achieved.

BUCHANAN AND THE COURT

An even more abrasive argument erupted between the president and secretary of state on May 13, 1846, as war with Mexico was about to be declared. Buchanan told the cabinet that he wanted to advise foreign governments, especially Britain and France, that the United States had no aim to seize California. Polk, who of course had every intention of taking California, sharply told his secretary not to deliver any such message. Buchanan pushed him, warning that unless he reassured Britain and France about it, there could be war with both of them.

Polk exploded: "Before I would make a pledge like that I would meet the war with England or France or all the powers of Christendom . . . and that I would stand and fight until the last man."[54]

The contentious relationship between James K. Polk and James Buchanan is mystifying and raises questions as to why they did not end it. Buchanan without doubt was more politician than diplomat, constantly testing the winds blowing in Congress and bringing baggage to cabinet meetings from his wide range of political contacts. Polk confessed in the diary that he knew his secretary of state had violated his rule against politicking and at one point said he would be happy if Buchanan quit. Then, when he had a chance to get rid of him, the president backed away. In June 1846 Buchanan met with Polk and asked to be named to the U.S. Supreme Court. After three conversations Polk and Buchanan dropped the matter. The diary reads as if Polk did not want him to go.

Even these affable chats about the possibility of Buchanan joining the judiciary led to another hurtful scene between them. On deciding to stay in the cabinet, Buchanan pushed the president to name a political ally, John M. Read of Philadelphia, to the Court. And why not? Read had supported Polk for president and was an outstanding lawyer. There is little doubt that Buchanan left the White House that day and told friends (and probably Read) to expect the appointment. Little did he understand his president.

Without any further conversation, Polk nominated George Woodward, a Pennsylvania state judge who was no friend of the secretary of state. Buchanan, his feelings badly damaged, made his way to the White House to grumble. He had lost two nights' sleep over the callous affront to his self-esteem, he told Polk. The president should have done him the courtesy of alerting him in advance that Read would not be appointed.

Polk bluntly told him, "As President of the United States I was responsible for my appointments and . . . I had a perfect right to make them without consulting with my cabinet, unless I desired their advice." Woodward, he had decided, was "the preferable man."[55] He was more forthcoming to his diary: "Mr. Read, I learned, until ten or twelve years ago was a leading Federalist. . . . I have never known an instance of a Federalist who had, after arriving at the age of thirty, professed to change his opinions. . . . I resolved to appoint no man who was not an original Democrat."[56]

The Senate killed Woodward's nomination to the Court, and Polk wrote in the diary that he suspected Buchanan had lobbied secretly against him. Given the constant unpleasantness between them, it is interesting to speculate why Polk retained Buchanan in his post to the very end of the administration. Perhaps recalling the time when Jackson played cabinet musical chairs, he wanted the image of stability in his administration. Polk had discovered that for all Buchanan's obstreperousness, he could control him. The historian Charles A. McCoy reasoned that "President Polk was able and willing to keep Buchanan in his Cabinet, for he never could dominate the President."[57] In Polk's mind Buchanan had the title, but *he* indeed was secretary of state.

6

War

In office a year and a half, the hard-driving president now had achieved three of the four goals he had set for himself. On June 15, 1846, he had reached agreement with the British on Oregon; six weeks later he signed the tariff bill into law; in August came passage of his Constitutional Treasury.

The only "great measure" remaining was the acquisition of California—and to succeed there he would have to win a war, battle with Congress, and barter with the enemy for the magnificent coastal strip.

It was the war that would define the Polk administration, for better and for worse. The acquisition of the California and New Mexico territories would bring accolades for completing the grand design of a continental nation stretching from ocean to ocean. George Bancroft spoke for those who supported the war when he said he considered "the acquisition of California by ourselves as the decisive point in the perfect establishment of the Union." Now the nation rested, he said, on "a foundation that cannot be moved."[1] Polk's critics characterized his war as the brutal conquest of a benighted, defenseless, vulnerable neighbor with little ability to defend itself. Initially, that dissent was led by the so-called Conscience Whigs, a small group mostly from Massachusetts, who saw in the conflict not only "the iniquity of aggression but the iniquity of its purpose—the spread of slavery."[2] In fairness to the fears of the Conscience Whigs, John C. Calhoun, as secretary of state under Tyler, had made no bones about his plan that Texas would enlarge the nation's slave territory. As a slave owner, Polk was suspect in the minds of these dissenters. In fairness to the president, he cared not whether Texas came in as a slave state or free. He passionately wanted Texas and would let the new state decide about slavery. With the same passion, slave or free, he wanted California.

The war ignited in April 1846 with a flourish of national patriotic fervor and public enthusiasm, an overwhelming "declaration of war" vote in both houses of Congress, and a rush of volunteers to join the army. Then, after a series of smashing military victories inside Mexico, the war dragged on for almost two years, casualties mounting, costs accelerating until Whig opposition in Congress, once a murmur, ultimately became an orchestrated chorus.

Polk had been quick to learn that there was no comparison between fighting and winning battles in Congress and fighting and winning a foreign war. It was frustrating in the extreme for a hands-on chief executive, immensely self-confident and completely involved in the workings of his government, to discover that there were events in war he could not control, mistakes he could not prevent, developments he could not manipulate. He was an armchair commander in chief, two thousand miles from the front, lacking direct communication with generals he did not trust and was powerless to manage.

There were other irritants. Newspaper dispatches from the war front sometimes conflicted with official reports. The Washington rumor mill, with its unofficial back-channel gossips, whose intelligence often was imagined, also confused on any day what Washington knew or thought it knew about war progress. Polk was further put off by the constant patronage demands from members of Congress who seemed willing to barter votes on legislation in return for military commissions for friends, relatives, and sometimes them-selves. From Polk's earliest days in the office he thought dispensing patronage was the most repulsive aspect of his job.

He now predicted that "patronage of the government will destroy the popularity of any President, however well he may administer the government."[3] Even cabinet members were expect-ing appointments for their friends. Marcy, who coined the telling phrase "to the victors belong the spoils," moaned whenever his Democratic enemies in New York won administration favors, and Buchanan always was out to best Vice President Dallas with regard to plums that went to the party faithful in Pennsylvania.[4]

POLK'S GENERALS

More upsetting than anything else was Polk's lack of confidence in the ability of his two ranking field commanders, Major General Winfield Scott and Brigadier General Zachary Taylor. While their military credentials were outstanding, their courage unquestioned, and their patriotism admirable, they both were Whigs—and both had political aspirations.

Nowhere does Polk's intense partisanship appear more obvious or more wrongheaded than in his diary comments about Taylor and Scott. His extensive musings about their Whig leanings reflected a vindictiveness that sometimes was petty and bordered on irra-tional. Both generals won repeated victories over the Mexican army in the field, but back in Washington, jumping to conclusions at long distance, Polk judged them harshly. At one point in November 1846 there was an outburst in his diary in which he described Taylor as "ungrateful," "narrow-minded," "bigoted," and "partisan."[5] Three months later he called Scott "arbitrary," "pro-scriptive," and "tyrannical"[6] for disciplining a subordinate officer who was a Democrat. These were not incidental comments. He routinely criticized them to the cabinet and in the diary.

He was right about their politics. They were Whigs. And he was right about their ambitions. Both would use their war records to run for president. Taylor and Scott became as suspicious of their partisan president as he was of them. There came a time when Taylor, convinced that "Polk, Marcy and Co." were out to "discredit and ruin" him, violated the president's order to remain in Monterrey, then pushed on to a magnificent victory at Buena Vista.[7]

The fact that the generals were political did not make them inept battle commanders. Indeed, military historians have judged them able and effective. Some experts on warfare consider Scott, a West Point graduate, the most gifted military strategist of his time. The successes of both men in Mexico attest to their qualifications as military leaders.

If Polk could have done it (and he seriously considered it), he would have replaced them both with a supergeneral of his personal preference who was a Democrat. He had Senator Thomas Hart Benton, Old Bullion, in mind for that lofty post, but after testing congressional waters on the idea, he found little support for it and dropped it. His friend Gideon Pillow, who had been his law partner, understood the battle strategy of a national convention but had no experience in a shooting war. He asked for a commission, and Polk, who had refused the friends of others, had no reluctance giving his old friend a patronage gift. He named Pillow brigadier general, then elevated him to major general, an appointment and promotion seen within the military as blatant favoritism. Pillow demonstrated considerable ability as a leader in battle, but his rank was viewed as sleeveless by his fellow officers.

Polk was typically self-righteous in a November 1846 diary entry: "I stated what all the Cabinet knew, that I had never suffered politics to mingle with the conduct of the war."[8] Every cabinet officer probably would have sworn to it—and would have sworn falsely.

Both Scott and Taylor came to understand that the commander in chief's censorious feelings toward them were grounded in their ambitions, not in their faults as soldiers. By the time war broke out, Scott already was being urged to seek the Whig nomination. It would be Taylor, however, who won favor at the 1848 Whig convention and then succeeded Polk as president. Scott would take the Whig nomination in 1852 and lose to Franklin Pierce. The Mexican war made Taylor the new national hero.

Stressful relations had simmered between the United States and Mexico for a decade. The brutality of the assaults at the Alamo and Goliad in 1836 was still fresh in the national memory. In addition, U.S. citizens had more than $3 million in legitimate claims against the Mexican government, which were in default. Across the border, the Mexican mind-set was seething anger. The Texas revolution had been led and waged by men who had come westward from the United States, robbing Mexicans of their land and their pride. Sam Houston, the hated general who had defeated their army at San Jacinto later in 1836, was known to be the close friend and former Tennessee congressional colleague of Polk, the U.S. president.

Polk's inaugural address sent a clear message to the Mexicans. He would weld Texas to the Union—and nobody had a right to resent it. "I regard the question of annexation as belonging exclusively to the United States and Texas," he said. Foreign powers should appreciate that this was no "conquest by a nation seeking to extend her domination by arms and violence, but . . . the peaceful acquisition of a territory once her own."[9] The Mexicans thought this territory was *their* own.

On March 28, three weeks after Polk's speech, Mexico formally broke off diplomatic relations with the United States. There was concern both in Washington and in Texas that Mexico might invade. Polk waited a month before sending William Parrott, a dentist who lived in Mexico, as his covert agent to see if the government of President José Joaquín de Herrera had cooled down and was willing to negotiate "in a liberal and friendly spirit."[10] Dr. Parrott, whose mission was kept secret, sent back the bad news that Herrera seemed ready to go to war over Texas and was unwilling to negotiate.

On June 15, as tensions heightened, Polk followed the advice of his cabinet and directed General Taylor to move his army of three thousand men to Corpus Christi, within a day's march from the Rio Grande. Here U.S. forces were walking into what Polk's Whig opponents would come to call "disputed" land. It was "disputed" because after Sam Houston won the Texas revolution and crushed the Mexicans at San Jacinto, the defeated general, Antonio López de Santa Anna, had agreed that the new Texas-Mexico border was the Rio Grande. The Mexican Congress later repudiated that agreement, but Texans—and Polk—claimed all the territory between the Nueces and Rio Grande rivers. In sending General Taylor into this area, Polk advised him that if Mexican troops crossed the Rio Grande he was to consider it "the commencement of hostilities."[11] On August 29 Polk ordered Secretary Marcy to direct Taylor to be prepared, if attacked by Mexican troops, to drive them back across the Rio Grande and seize Matamoras and any other enemy base in the proximity of the river.

From December 29, 1845, when Texas was admitted to the Union as the twenty-eighth state, a warlike mentality took root in Mexico and grew over four months to the point that, by April, Polk and his cabinet were expecting an attack. It came on April 24, when mounted Mexican soldiers ambushed a scouting troop under Taylor's command on the "Texas side" of the Rio Grande, killing eleven and wounding two. The general, following orders from Polk and Marcy, and regarding the assault "an act of war,"[12] immediately was spurred into action. He crossed the Rio with two thousand men and went after the enemy. His men called Taylor "Old Rough and Ready." A folk hero was in the making.

By the time the president had learned of the conflict on May 9, and Congress declared war four days later, Taylor had seized Mattamoras and, outnumbered two to one, had pushed on to win bloody battles at Palo Alto and Resaca de la Palma. His casualties

were relatively light: approximately 170 killed and wounded.
Mexico suffered 800 dead and wounded.

By September, the general had pushed north and captured
Monterrey, again after heavy fighting against a larger army. His
most notable feat, executed after he violated Polk's order to
remain at Monterrey, came in February 1847 at Buena Vista,
where his troops, outmanned four to one—20,000 to 5,000—
routed the Mexicans. When it was over, the United States had 272
slain, 387 wounded, and 6 missing. The Mexican dead numbered
591, the wounded 1,048, and the missing 1,800. Taylor's dramatic
victories led Polk to elevate him to major general, although the
president was furious that the general had ignored his command
and moved from Monterrey.

The president was saddened to learn that among those who fell
at Buena Vista was his old friend Colonel Archibald Yell. Like
Cave Johnson, John Catron, and Aaron Brown, Yell had been an
intimate colleague during those years he had served as a Tennessee
legislator, federal judge, and governor of Arkansas. "It was a severe
battle," Polk wrote in his diary. He mourned Yell as "a brave and
good man, and among the best friends I had on earth." Yell's oldest
son was a student at Georgetown, and since his friend had "died
poor," the president said he would "educate the boy and . . . take
great interest in him."

Buena Vista had been a risky battle but a stunning victory. Still
Polk could not bring himself to praise the general even in the pri-
vacy of his daily log. The success in conflict had nothing to do with
Taylor's generalship, he said, but "was due to the indomitable and
intrepid bravery of the officers and men under his command." He
continued to verbally lash the general. His "rashness" in disobeying
orders to remain in Monterrey had been responsible for the tragic
loss of "many valuable officers." Taylor was "a hard fighter," Polk concluded, "but has none of the other qualities of a great general."[13]

By this time the relentless micromanager was nitpicking Taylor's method of supplying his troops. He sought out General T. S.

Jesup, stationed in Washington, and suggested that Taylor was guilty of a serious blunder in transporting supplies through Mexico by wagon train. Would it not be better to use mules? The general gave his "decided opinion" that baggage wagons should be dispensed with and mules employed. That night Polk confided in his diary, "General Taylor, I fear, is not the man for the command of the army. He is brave but . . . I think him unfit for the chief command."[14] His problem, he said, was that he had no one else to put in charge—and Taylor was popular.

By the beginning of 1847 the commander in chief was convinced that the new national hero was "wholly incompetent for so large a command."[15] In mid-January he recorded this: "The truth is, neither Taylor nor Scott are fit for the command of the army."[16] The president could degrade Taylor in cabinet meetings and ridicule him in his diary entries, but in the public mind Old Rough and Ready had become a revered celebrity. After the war, when Taylor, still an army general, first was mentioned as a Whig candidate for president, Polk was livid and delivered the ultimate insult. "General Taylor is a Whig alias Federalist of the most decided character."[17]

THE WAR FROM WASHINGTON

Winfield Scott got off to an even more unpleasant start with the president than did his subordinate. The president anticipated that Scott, as the nation's top-ranked general, would rush at once to Mexico, but a week after hostilities commenced he was still sitting at his desk in Washington telling friends that he would not be needed at the front until September. The president got wind of the rumors and told Marcy to get the general out of Washington and on his way south of the border. "Take the matter into your own hands," he told the secretary of war. "Issue his orders and cause them to be obeyed."[18] Scott reacted badly. He fired off a letter to Marcy. "I do not desire to place myself in the most perilous of all positions—a fire upon my rear from Washington, and the fire, in front, from the Mexicans."[19] The general, endowed with an enlarged ego perhaps not matched in American military history until the coming of Douglas MacArthur, had challenged his civilian commander in chief—who let him know, Truman-like, who was boss. Polk summarily removed him from command, grounding him in the capital.

Deprived of a field generalship, Scott was searching for a way back into the administration's favor. By September, the time Scott originally had said he would go to the front, the president noted that the burdens of war were wearing heavily on Marcy, but added, "General Scott is of no aid to the department. . . . His presence at Washington is constantly embarrassing to the Secretary of War."[20] That was about to change. Aware that the cabinet was discussing the possibility of an attack across the Gulf of Mexico on Veracruz, Scott drafted three innovative memoranda for Marcy detailing plans for taking the coastal city, then pushing across country, capturing Mexico City, and bringing an end to the war. Marcy, keenly aware of Polk's mistrust of Scott, began to lobby other members of the cabinet for the general's plan, and, on October 22, with Taylor temporarily holding Monterrey, Marcy raised the subject of the Veracruz initiative with the president. Polk reported in his diary, "The Secretary of War read a written memorandum from General Scott giving a statement of the forces now in Mexico and the additional forces and preparations which in his opinion would be necessary to make an attack on . . . Vera Cruz and march to the City of Mexico."[21]

Scott said it would require fourteen thousand men—although earlier he had suggested it might take twice that number. The cabinet listened, and Marcy, Mason, Buchanan, and Walker all favored Scott as commanding officer for the expedition. Only Cave Johnson, perhaps reading the president's mind, was opposed. "I have strong objections to General Scott," Polk reported that night. "Nothing but stern necessity and a sense of duty could induce me to place him at the head of so important an expedition." He acknowledged, however, that Scott was "General-in-chief of the Army" and concluded, "I do not well see how it can be avoided."[22]

It was the right choice. It took four months to amass the thirty thousand volunteers and regulars, a substantial number peeled off Taylor's army, for the assault on Veracruz. It came in late March, and by month's end Scott had crossed the Gulf of Mexico and captured the city. Over the next six months his army rolled inland toward the Mexican capital. In successive order he would take and pacify Cerro Gordo, Cherubusco, and Contreras, then Molino del Rey, Chapultepec, and, on September 14, Mexico City. Still, nothing Scott did in the field deserved positive mention in Polk's diary. At one point the armchair commander concluded after a guerrilla attack that "General Scott had left his rear unprotected."[23] Again he blamed "the protraction of the war" on Scott's "folly and ridiculous vanity."[24] After Mexico City's conquest, the war effectively was over. Polk's two Whig generals had done it.

There was at least one Whig officer in whom Polk placed great trust. Stephen W. Kearney had no interest in running for political office, although he was to prove to be able to take care of himself in military politics. To Colonel Kearney, the president entrusted the Army of the West, assigning him, soon after Congress declared war, the duty of moving a force westward to protect traders and settlers along the way to Santa Fe. He then pushed on to California. By the time he raised the flag over Santa Fe, Colonel Kearney was a brigadier general, an indication of the importance the commander in chief placed on Kearney's role in the resolution of the war. The president may have been preoccupied with the reports from Scott in Veracruz and Taylor in Monterrey, but California was never far from his mind. As the historian K. Jack Bauer points out, "He viewed possession as a weapon to force the Mexicans into a general boundary and claims settlement."[25] And possession of California was a major goal. George Bancroft, who was appointed secretary of the navy on March 10, only a week after

Polk became president, was alerting his fleet to the prospect of moving in on San Francisco from the sea even before Mexico broke diplomatic relations. Only ten days in office, Bancroft shot off a dispatch to Commodore John D. Sloat, his commander in the Pacific: "Should you ascertain beyond a doubt that the Mexican government has declared war against us, you will at once . . . possess yourself of the port of San Francisco, and blockade or occupy . . . other ports."[26]

As it turned out, Sloat, though cautious, in poor health, and eager to retire, moved in on northern California in June and, aware that war had been declared, captured Monterey with 250 marines and sailors from the frigate *Savannah*. A British warship, the *Juno*, was anchored in the bay as the occupation occurred. The Stars and Stripes was raised over San Francisco by men from his companion ship, the *Portsmouth*, two days later. The United States had "possession." From that point Polk had a military claim on the land he most desired.

There would be skirmishes and clashes with Mexican troops in California, both by the naval forces under Commodore Robert Stockton, to whom Sloat relinquished command, and by the army under General Kearney, who assumed authority over California, as Polk had directed him. An unfortunate clash of personalities between Kearney and Stockton was about to occur over military leadership, and Kearney would win that battle, too.

POLK AND FRÉMONT

It was a raw power struggle between General Kearney and Commodore Stockton, as the conquest of California was assured. An unfortunate political casualty of their conflict was Colonel John C. Frémont, the famed Oregon pathfinder and son-in-law of Senator Thomas Hart Benton, the powerful Missouri Democrat.

K. Jack Bauer wrote:

After the fall of Los Angeles the long-brewing confrontation between Kearney and Stockton over political control of California finally developed. Stockton claimed exclusive control . . . because of his prior possession. . . . The clash came into the open on January 16 [1847] when Stockton issued Frémont a commission as Governor of California. Kearney immediately demanded that Stockton cease the formation of a civil government.[27]

Colonel Frémont, loyal to Stockton and enamored with the title of "governor," immediately advised Kearney that he would accept no orders from him. No doubt, he was relying on Benton's political muscle in Washington to help him in his fight with the general in California. After all, the Missouri senator, for all his bombast, repeatedly had demonstrated friendship for Polk and had been a valuable adviser on many issues. Frémont knew, of course, that early in the war the president briefly considered commissioning Benton supreme commanding general. And so the "governor" continued to defy Kearney until finally, in March, in refusing another order, Frémont challenged Colonel Richard Mason, the general's subordinate, to a duel. It was never fought, but the result was a court-martial at which Frémont was found guilty of mutiny and insubordination.

Most of the president's cabinet, friendly to Benton, would have been content had the president cleared Frémont of all charges. But the arbitrary streak that so often moved Polk to deal with friends as distantly as enemies took hold. Aware that any mark on Frémont's record would upset Benton, Polk upheld the lesser count of insubordination, while dismissing the mutiny charge. He restored Frémont to duty, but the pathfinder resigned in anger and moved with his wife to California. Three months later Polk noted with a twinge of regret that he had lost Benton as a friend. On the occasional Sundays when he attended services with Sarah he would see the Missouri senator, who, he said, "never speaks to me."[28] Polk's self-righteousness returned, however, when he was handed a press report that Benton had advised California residents to form their own government while waiting for Congress to admit them to the Union. Polk, outraged, had postal authorities send out notices to the western territories declaring that they had no right to self-government. Soon he would be sending another message to the nation about California: Gold had been discovered there. As he was leaving office, the lure of riches accelerated the rush to California and hastened statehood. When it came in 1850, one of the state's first two senators would be John C. Frémont. By then Polk was in his grave.

THE BACK DOOR

It had taken skill, manpower, courage, and luck, but the fighting war, while wearing on the national psyche, had gone well. The diplomatic initiatives to end the war were less impressive. Somewhere in Polk's mind was the idea that a stick-and-carrot approach would bring an early end to hostilities. If the military strikes were bold and effective, he thought, perhaps he could purchase peace and claim California. He was wrong. Mexican antagonism did not dissipate after the Herrera government was overthrown by General Paredes. Polk badly misjudged the will and pride of the Mexicans and their enmity for the United States—a miscalculation of an enemy not to be repeated until the Vietnam War. Finally, it dawned on Polk that there would be no diplomatic quick fix to end the conflict.

It was the president's policy of leaving the door to the White House open for visits by total strangers that brought on the next abortive diplomatic scheme. It was Friday the thirteenth of February when the president found himself closeted with an unlikely caller on an unlikely mission: A. J. Atocha, a native Spaniard who had become an American citizen, had been a close friend of the deposed and banished Mexican dictator Antonio López de Santa

Anna, the villain of the Alamo. According to Atocha, Santa Anna, then in exile in Havana, was eager to return to Mexico and take control of the nation. If he could do so, Atocha said, Santa Anna would negotiate a settlement between his country and the United States that would satisfy Polk. The president noted in his diary that he did not trust Atocha. But he did listen to him. Six months later Commodore David Conner, acting on specific instructions from Washington, allowed Santa Anna to slip through the blockade at Veracruz and reenter Mexico. Once the wily Santa Anna was home, he seized power and gave Polk every reason to know he had been right not to trust Atocha. Santa Anna fought ferociously in a series of battles against first Taylor and then Scott and would not negotiate until after the fall of Mexico City.

If intransigence marked the Mexican mood, ambivalence took hold in the United States as the war wore on. On one side there was the the antiwar protest movement. On the other was the drive to grab all of Mexico as the successes of Taylor, Scott, and Kearney became heralded. The question was, should the United States simply annex all of Mexico? The Democrats' loss of the House of Representatives in Polk's midterm came, as the political scientist Frederick Merk pointed out, "in the midst of a highly successful war." It was "a clear measure of the moral protest which had developed against the war."[29] In that political campaign Whig candidates had raised the question whether Polk had misled Congress at the war's outset by claiming that the assault on Taylor's ambushed troop occurred on "our soil."

Abraham Lincoln, the young congressman from Illinois, argued on the House floor that the blood was spilled on "disputed" territory. Certainly the territory was disputed. Texas claimed it; Mexico did as well. In fact, the Mexican government had never recognized the Republic of Texas. As Merk said, constant criticism of the war by political Whigs, together with constant praise and support for Taylor and Scott, the Whig generals, was good politics in 1846. It was grounded in growing public disenchantment with the costs and casualties of conflict. Unlike the leaders in the later unpopular Vietnam War, the Polk administration admitted it saw no light at the end of the tunnel. After twenty months, Congressman Lincoln said of Polk, "As to the end, he himself has [not] even an imaginary conception."[30]

Almost 13,000 men had died, 11,000 from disease, accidents, and noncombat causes, and more than 1,700 from battle wounds. When it started, there were 637 officers commanding nearly 6,000 enlisted men. At the end, regular army ranks were swollen to almost 43,000, and another 73,000 were listed as volunteers in state units.

It was that handful of Conscience Whigs, led by John Quincy Adams, that had initially condemned the war as unjust. Pain over the loss of life and treasure added to a building sentiment of moral outrage as more people came to the view of those early dissenters: war fought solely for expansionist aims was ethically indefensible. Adams himself would not live to see ratification of the treaty ending the war he had so opposed. The cannon fire had ceased, but the armistice had not yet been consummated, when he died on February 23, 1848, after collapsing on the floor of the House. President Polk ordered all flags at half-mast and attended the memorial service two days later at the Capitol. He was appropriately respectful in his diary but did not feign deep regret that the antiwar voice of his eighty-one-year-old critic was stilled.

Other voices had joined the protests. Henry David Thoreau's challenging essay "Civil Disobedience" and the biting satire of James Russell Lowell's *Bigelow Papers* fed this intellectual angst. Ralph Waldo Emerson said, "The United States will conquer Mexico, but it will be as the man swallows arsenic. . . . Mexico will poison us."[31] For many who wrote of the war in later generations, the thrust of the arguments of the Conscience Whigs stuck. Robert Kennedy, speaking in Indonesia in early 1962, responded to a student's question by saying, "I don't think that this is a very bright page in American history."[32] His comment made the news wires and brought a blast of criticism from Vice President Lyndon Johnson, who thought it was a bright page, indeed.

There was clear evidence of hotly divided public opinion on the war. In the angry heat that followed the first American bloodshed, the declaration of war passed the House by an overpowering margin of 174 to 14. (The Senate went for it 40 to 2.) In January 1848, however, the House, by a vote of 82 to 81, denounced the conflict as "a war unnecessarily and unconstitutionally begun by the President of the United States."[33]

Lincoln's attack on the war came shortly after that vote. It was applauded by his eighty Whig colleagues in the House but did not go down well at home in Illinois, where sentiment favoring the war was strong. The historian Bernard De Voto said that this speech and his general antiwar record "retired Lincoln to private life."[34] It was hardly permanent retirement.

His words demanding that Polk tell Congress exactly "the spot" where the blood had been spilled effectively accused Polk of dishonesty and must have discomfited the president. The irony is that some of what Lincoln said also came to cause *him* discomfort when he was in the White House. "Any people anywhere," he declared in defense of Texas's armed revolution, "have the right to rise up, and shake off the existing government, and form one that suits them better."[35] It was a right he later would deny existed for the Confederate States of America. In fact, his pacific views on Polk's war also would put him at sharp odds with the theory of anticipatory self-defense espoused by America's forty-third president, George W. Bush, as a justification of his plans to invade Iraq. Polk had no right to send Taylor into Mexico, Lincoln declared. "Allow the President to invade a neighboring nation, whenever he shall deem it necessary to repel an invasion . . . and you allow him to make war at pleasure."[36]

If the votes of eighty-two congressmen against the conflict were a measure of intense antiwar sentiment, the votes of eighty-one others reflect the clear and sharp division of opinion in the country. While conquest had dulled the taste of many citizens, it whetted the appetite of many others who saw Taylor holding Buena Vista, Scott moving on Mexico City, and Kearney raising the flag over New Mexico and California. Why settle for Polk's demand for a piece of northern California and a border at the Rio Grande? Why not all of Mexico? "All Mexico" now became a movement that gathered its own momentum as the reality of conquest merged with the mood of Manifest Destiny.[37]

Senator Sidney Breese of Illinois won praise from Lincoln's home-state critics when he raised his voice for All Mexico, both to acquire its wealth of natural resources and to bring the Mexican people "under the happy influences" of American civil and religious liberties.[38] Secretary of State Buchanan and Secretary of the Treasury Walker found themselves under the expansionist spell of this All-Mexico mentality, joined by Vice President Dallas, for once in agreement with Buchanan.

Walt Whitman said, "Every body knows we can take possession of the country. . . . We must hold possession and so manage that they stay beat."[39] From Europe Karl Marx and Friedrich Engels, whose expansionist ideas would take another part of the world in a different direction, both endorsed the U.S. conquest. Marx, with sarcasm, asked if "it was such a misfortune that glorious California has been wrenched from lazy Mexicans."[40] There was suddenly wide support in the Senate for "annexation" of all of Mexico. Senator Daniel Dickinson of New York envisioned "a more perfect Union: embracing the entire North American continent."[41] Senator Ambrose Sevier of Arkansas thought that the "degraded" Mexicans could be uplifted by "American laws, education and kindness."[42] Sam Houston had his own moral take on the idea: "The Divine Being has been evidently carrying out the destiny of the American race" to civilize the continent.[43]

Polk, battered by the war protests and tempted by the All-Mexico advocates, stayed to his course. He wanted peace, California, and the Rio Grande border—and was willing to pay $20 million for it.

THE WILMOT PROVISO

Polk's frequent requests to Congress for money to supply the growing regular army had met with approval. Most congressmen who
voted against his war as unnecessary and unconstitutional, Lincoln
among them, would not vote to deny Scott, Taylor, and Kearney
anything. The president asked for an appropriation of $2 million as
a good-faith down payment when Mexico came to the table, as he
was sure Santa Anna would. Approval seemed certain.

Then on August 8, 1846, word came to the White House that
while his request for the funds had been approved in the House, an
amendment by Representative David Wilmot of Pennsylvania, an
abolitionist, had been added requiring that "neither slavery nor
involuntary servitude shall ever exist"[44] in any territory acquired
from Mexico. Polk had gagged the slavery debate in Congress when
he was Speaker, but now he was president and would have to deal
with Wilmot. The amendment was "mischievous and foolish," he
recorded in his diary. "What connection slavery had with making
peace with Mexico is difficult to conceive."[45] He rallied support in
the Senate and with Calhoun's unsolicited support killed the
amendment. It would, he suspected, be revived by Wilmot in the
next session, and Polk hoped to head it off by convincing the Pennsylvania congressman that it was imprudent.

Just before Christmas, Polk invited Wilmot to the White House
to talk about it. "I told him I did not desire to extend slavery, that I
would be satisfied to acquire . . . from Mexico [as free territories]
the Provinces of New Mexico and the Californias." He added that
"in these Provinces slavery could probably never exist. . . . The
great probability was that the question would never arise."[46]

Polk explained to the congressman that if his proviso remained as
part of the legislation, "every Senator from a slave-holding state"[47]
would oppose it and it would be defeated. Wilmot understood. He
told Polk he was willing to support the $2 million appropriation
without the amendment, but that if some other congressman intro-

duced it, he would vote for it. Of course the amendment was reintroduced in the next session—and the war dragged on while Congress wrangled. Of all the members of the Senate, Calhoun was the most offended by Wilmot's rider. He was the most rabid of states' rights advocates but saw no inconsistency in seeking to have the federal government impose slavery on future states. With less than two months remaining in the White House, Young Hickory received a visit on January 16 from Calhoun.

> I anticipated his business the moment he entered my office, and I was not mistaken. He very soon introduced the subject of the slavery question and the meeting of the Southern members of Congress at the Capitol last night. He was very earnest in the expression of his opinion that the South should no longer delay resisting the aggressions of the North upon their rights. I expressed my strong attachment to the Union of the States, the great importance of preserving it, and my hope that governments might be provided for California and New Mexico . . . without . . . the Wilmot Proviso.[48]

That would mean "the question of slavery would be left to the people of the new State."[49]

Polk also told Calhoun that continued agitation about slavery was "delicate and dangerous . . . (and) should be arrested." Calhoun didn't like what he heard. "He proposed no plan of adjusting the difficulty. . . . I was firm and decided in my conversation with him," said Polk. "I gave no countenance to any movement which tended to violence or disunion of the States."[50]

Here was Polk at his best. The confrontation finds him opposed to the arbitrary extension of slavery to new states and hostile to Calhoun's talk of "action" against fellow citizens in the North. Polk would have none of that. He was for the Union. His faith in that simple Jacksonian doctrine was unshakable, almost religious. His stance with Calhoun does him credit. After Jackson, he

battled more strenuously than any other leader of his time to pre-
serve national unity in the face of intense divisive pressures
imposed by the proponents of slavery.

That said, he knew well enough that slavery was a "common
evil," yet he remained silent on the immorality and injustice of it.
It was not as if the people of his home state universally endorsed
it. By the time he was admitted to the bar, Tennessee abolitionists
were circulating *The Emancipator,* the nation's second antislavery
publication, and by the time he was in Congress there were at
least twenty-five manumission societies across his state, whose
members decried the depravity of the institution. While it would
have been political suicide to echo manumission rhetoric as a candidate, he was a four-year, one-term president by choice. There
came a time late in his term when he could have spoken out with
no risk.

Five short months after that meeting with Calhoun, Polk was
buried in Nashville. In his will he left all his slaves to Sarah for her
lifetime, after which they were to be freed. Unfortunately for the
slaves, she lived another forty-two years. Lincoln, however, had by
then long since emancipated them, and Tennessee had ratified the
Thirteenth Amendment outlawing slavery before her death.

7

Polk at Peace

As Polk was presiding over a nation tired of war, so was the devious Santa Anna, who, allowed back into his country to make peace, had only made war. His army was shattered, his treasury drained, and his people in pain. Peace came by a strange twist of circumstances as a result of the efforts of a negotiator, Nicholas Trist, a State Department bureaucrat who was first designated, and then fired, by Polk. Trist simply refused to quit when the president discharged him. Finally, he reached an acceptable deal with the Mexican dictator.

Trist had been Buchanan's chief clerk at the State Department, and it was the secretary who urged the president to pick him for the trying task of talking through an agreement with the enemy. His first effort produced a proposal from Santa Anna in late August that was far short of what Polk expected. At that point, feeling great disappointment, the president promptly sent word to Trist that he was dismissed. The State Department clerk, believing he was closer to a more positive resolution than Polk understood, continued to negotiate, urged on by General Scott, who remained in Mexico City.

At this point, in the absence of action with the enemy, Generals Scott and Pillow went to war with each other over who deserved credit for the Mexico City campaign. The hostilities were carried on through exchanges of correspondence that included charges and countercharges that were little more than poison-pen letters by two ego-driven personalities. There were hearings and investigations, but these were resolved without any findings of guilt. Polk, of course, exonerated Pillow, his former law partner, and blamed his general in chief for his "arrogance and inordinate vanity."[1] He again removed Scott from command.

Polk had been agitated when Trist refused to come home, but when the president received the new proposal from the Mexicans dated January 31, he found it acceptable. The two governments entered into a treaty in February, almost two years after the Mexicans had ambushed Taylor's dragoons in the disputed territory just north of the Rio Grande. Not until the Gulf of Tonkin incident in the Vietnam War would such a querulous dispute puzzle the American citizens in an unpopular war.

Under the agreement, Mexico abandoned any claims on California and New Mexico and gave up clear title to the land north of the Rio Grande—more than a half-million square miles. In return, the administration agreed to pay Mexico $15 million plus take on assumption of the $3 million in American citizens' claims against Mexico. On March 10 the Senate ratified the treaty by a vote of 38 to 14. Polk's "short war" was over.

Condemnation of the war robbed Polk of the opportunity to be judged more kindly by history. The conflict took its toll on the nation—and on the president. The combined attacks, often exaggerated, from the Whigs and those who condemned the war, charged him with an exercise in imperialist militarism—crushing an impotent army and raping a helpless land.

LEGACY

Polk had done all that he set out to do. He was ready to go home to Tennessee. The challenges were less intense during the last months in office. Still, the workaholic president did little but work. In November 1848 the Whigs, having nominated General Taylor, elected him over Lewis Cass and a surprise third-party Free Soil candidate, Martin Van Buren. Polk expressed patronizing pity for Van Buren, but his view of Taylor as a presidential prospect was identical to his judgment of him as a general of the army: "He is wholly unqualified."[2]

At the end, members of the Polk cabinet wondered whether they should call on the new president as a matter of courtesy. When Buchanan asked the question, Polk, for one last time, put the secretary of state in his place. "I then informed him . . . that if my Cabinet called on General Taylor before he called on me, I should feel that I had been deserted by my own political family."[3] He learned a few days later that, once again, Buchanan had been offended. Polk took one final shot at him in his diary: "He is an able man . . . but sometimes he acts like an old maid."[4]

The final days were tiring. Taylor did come to call. Polk received hordes of visitors, and there was a final reception. He felt at times harassed by the flood of Whigs who had come to town to witness the changing of the guard. When he and Sarah started the long trip home, he was spent, wan, and appeared much older than his fifty-three years. He had purchased the home of his old law mentor, Felix Grundy, within sight of the state Capitol at Nashville, where he and Sarah would retire and rest.

He was ill virtually the entire monthlong trip home. He expressed concern at Mobile and New Orleans about a wave of cholera but said he thought his sickness, "a derangement of the stomach and bowels,"[5] perhaps would protect him from the dread disease. The last leg of his journey was by boat on the Cumberland River. A large crowd turned out on April 2 to welcome him. The official greeting came from Governor Aaron Brown, his oldest friend. The last thought in his diary that night was a cheerful acknowledgment that meeting old acquaintances had excited him and enabled him to "bear the fatigue" of the day.[6] Six weeks later he was dead.

Historians often have judged James Knox Polk as a pedantic, pompous, priggish chief of state. There is a puzzling contradiction here. In every poll taken since Arthur Schlesinger, Sr., began periodic surveys in 1948, experts have rated him consistently among the great and near-great presidents. John F. Kennedy was surprised to find Polk ranked ninth in the 1962 survey, below less activist presidents, such as Woodrow Wilson and Theodore Roosevelt, and once wondered whether historians—or anyone who had not served in the office—were qualified to judge presidential performance.

Presidential greatness is a term of elusive and elastic definition. It generally is conceded that presidents who combine a mesmeric personality with dynamic performance in times of crises are accorded the honorific. Their actions merge with their images to project an aura of public confidence, appreciation, and affection. Polk suffers because historians instinctively measure his accomplishments, which were substantial, alongside his presidential personality, which was anal. They discover in his diary a quixotic human whose writings and thought processes range from vanilla to venomous. As a result, they often describe him in derisive terms.

Polk was "colorless, methodical, plodding [and] narrow," said Allan Nevins.[7] "Puritanical" and "inflexible," according to Sam W. Haynes.[8] "A stern task-master" and "a loner," wrote Thomas M. Leonard.[9] "Not well-liked" and a "chilly demeanor," said Mark E. Byrnes.[10] He "lacked personal magnetism" and "developed no personal following," wrote Charles A. McCoy.[11] "Sometimes unscrupulous," according to Robert Remini.[12] He "had no humor," said Bernard De Voto.[13] Paul H. Bergeron noted "a seeming lack of candor and forthrightness."[14] To his wife's biographer, John Reed Bumgarner, he was "stiff, formal."[15] One of his biographers, Eugene

McCormac, called him "secretive—even sly."[16] And Charles Sellers, who wrote the definitive two-volume biography, found him "introverted and unrelaxed."[17]

"Lovable, or even likable, he was not," said Sellers.[18] And still there are moments when his diary reveals caring regard for family members, particularly his brothers, who all were younger and all but one of whom predeceased him. There also are flashes of a man with a good and generous heart. On a May Sunday in 1846, as he and Sarah walked from the executive residence on the way to church, they were confronted by a young man who was the son of a former law partner. He was down on his luck, ill, and emaciated. Polk gave him five dollars, had him fed at the White House, and arranged his stay at a hotel until his family could be contacted. Again, in November 1847 Felix Grundy's grandson, William Bass, turned up at his door broke and without a place to stay after he had dropped out of a college in Maryland. Polk put him up at the White House until relatives sent help.

Another gracious moment ended in tragedy. In September 1846, Representative Felix McConnell of Alabama, just recovering from a "fit of intoxication," asked Polk to lend him one hundred dollars to pay off some debts.[19] The next day the congressman was found dead in his hotel room, his throat cut, an obvious suicide. Shortly before McConnell went to his room, he let the hotel bartender borrow thirty-five dollars of the money Polk had given him.

His charity, however, had limits. He was infuriated when constantly badgered for contributions to diverse charities. "The idea seems to prevail," he said, "that the President is . . . compelled to contribute to every loafer who applies, provided he . . . wants to build a church, an academy, or a college." He complained that if he gave to all, he would be "utterly bankrupt."[20]

Polk left office with no iconic image, no host of hero-worshipers, no hordes of admirers sated with his charisma. If his administration approached "greatness"—and most of the writers cited above agree that it did—it was on the basis of performance alone.

His achievements, in the face of powerful congressional opposition at every turn, were nothing short of remarkable, changing forever the geography and the economy of the country. To achieve it all probably required a president who was partisan, demanding, determined, and even self-righteous. The Whig attacks that came late in his term, even in the face of his victory in the war, stung him and colored history's view of him. Perhaps he thought that his diary would provide the strong defense by which he would be remembered.

What Polk recorded about himself immeasurably enriches our understanding of his term in office. At the same time, it puts him under a looking glass with human flaws and personality quirks and sometimes makes him the author of his own disparagement. What he wrote in his diary often attests to his smallness as a human being. What he did in four hellish years attests to the greatness of his achievements.

Arthur Schlesinger, Jr., has compared Polk's standing among presidents with that of Harry Truman: "Neither Polk nor Truman was one of those creative presidents who make the nation look at things in a new way. . . . But both had the intelligence and courage to accept the challenge of history. History might have broken them, as it broke Buchanan and Hoover. Instead it forced them, not into personal greatness, but into the performance of great things."[21]

He did great things. That is a powerful epitaph.

Notes

INTRODUCTION: THE BORN-AGAIN PRESIDENT

1. Barber, p. 14.
2. Remini, *Andrew Jackson*, vol. 2, p. 89.
3. Schlesinger, *Age of Jackson*, p. 126.
4. Polk to Martin Van Buren, November 30, 1843, Polk correspondence.
5. Sellers, vol. 1, p. 490.
6. Cole, p. 390; Sellers, vol. 1, pp. 489–92.
7. Martin Van Buren to Polk, December 27, 1843, Polk correspondence.

1. THE BENT TWIG

1. Cook's essay in Meyers, p. 60.
2. Bancroft, p. 13.
3. McCormac, p. 2.
4. Tocqueville, vol. 1, pp. 319–20; vol. 2, p. 142.
5. *The Diary of James K. Polk*, October 14, 1846.
6. Ibid., April 6, 1848.
7. Ibid., August 26, 1845.
8. Polk inaugural address, p. 1.
9. *The Diary of James K. Polk*, November 2, 1845.

10. Ibid., November 2, 1848.
11. Ibid., January 31, 1846.
12. Ibid., May 19, 1846.
13. Ibid., October 14, 1846.
14. Ibid.
15. Ibid.
16. Sellers, vol. 1, p. 13.
17. *The Diary of James K. Polk*, October 18, 1848.
18. Bancroft, p. 3.
19. Author's interviews with Drs. Dean Knoll, Robert Ikard, Bernard Brody, Frank Boehm, and John Sergent, October–November 2002.
20. *The Diary of James K. Polk*, October 18, 1848.
21. Polk originally asked George Bancroft to write his official campaign biography, but when the historian could not find time and begged off, Polk relied on J. George Harris. Polk's biography was not printed as a pamphlet. Instead, the campaign widely distributed Harris's articles to friendly newspapers for reprint. Wayne Cutler, the historian heading the Polk Papers project at the University of Tennessee, found the *Union* articles during the course of his research and had them printed by the Tennessee Presidents Trust in 1990. Dr. Cutler believes the articles were dictated by Polk to Harris and read by him before publication.
22. Harris, p. 6.
23. Sellers reports that McDowell was the surgeon Sam wanted in the first place. According to his account, Sam heard that the Kentuckian had a heralded reputation for gallstone operations and set out with Jim from Columbia, for Danville. Since there was no gallstone operation performed in the United States until fifty-four years after Jim's surgery, and since the operation was for urinary stones, not gallstones, and since the campaign biography was based on interviews with Polk himself, the Harris account is reliable.
24. Ikard, p. 129.
25. Sellers, vol. 2, p. 42.
26. Ibid., p. 43.
27. Ibid., p. 47.

28. Ibid., p. 50.
29. Parks, p. 96.
30. Jenkins, pp. 48–49.
31. Harris, p. 9.
32. John S. Williamson to Polk, March 2, 1822, Polk correspondence.
33. William Polk to James K. Polk, February 17, 1821, Polk correspondence.
34. Polk to Samuel H. Laughlin, March 15, 1822, Polk correspondence.
35. Polk to William Polk, September 24, 1822, Polk correspondence.
36. Jesse W. Egnew to Polk, June 1820, Polk correspondence.
37. Sellers, vol. 1, p. 474.

2. OLD AND YOUNG HICKORY

1. Schlesinger, *Age of Jackson*, p. 37.
2. Ibid., p. 37, n. 11.
3. Ibid., p. 10.
4. Ibid., pp. 13, 268.
5. White, vol. 2, pp. 6, 7.
6. Sellers, vol. 1, p. 172.
7. Remini, *Andrew Jackson*, vol. 2, p. 48.
8. Jenkins, p. 57.
9. Sellers, vol. 1, p. 96.
10. Jenkins, p. 58.
11. McCormac, p. 14.
12. Ibid., p. 17.
13. Ibid., pp. 17–18.
14. Ibid., p. 19.
15. James K. Polk to William Polk, December 14, 1826, Polk correspondence.
16. Remini, *Henry Clay*, p. 292, citing letter from Henry Clay to John Crittenden, March 10, 1826.
17. Remini, *Andrew Jackson*, vol. 3, p. 122.
18. Remini, *Andrew Jackson*, vol. 2, p. 120, citing letter from Andrew Jackson to Sam Houston, December 15, 1826.

3. DEFENDER OF THE FAITH

1. Remini, *Andrew Jackson*, vol. 2, p. 161.
2. Ibid., p. 247.
3. Sellers, vol. 1, p. 153.
4. Ibid., p. 154.
5. Ibid.
6. Ibid., p. 155.
7. Schlesinger, *Age of Jackson*, p. 76.
8. Ibid., p. 9.
9. Ibid., p. 75.
10. Ibid., p. 89.
11. McCormac, p. 34, n. 14.
12. Polk to Francis Blair, August 8, 1833, Polk correspondence.
13. Ibid.
14. Ibid.
15. Remini, *Clay*, p. 445.
16. Remini, *Andrew Jackson*, vol. 3, p. 114.
17. Ibid., pp. 444–45.
18. Sellers, vol. 1, p. 217.
19. Ibid., p. 218.
20. Ibid., p. 217.
21. James Walker to Polk, October 22, 1833, Polk correspondence.
22. Remini, *Andrew Jackson*, vol. 3, p. 252.
23. Schlesinger, *Age of Jackson*, p. 129.
24. Sellers, vol. 1, p. 319.
25. Ibid., citing letter from Polk to William Warner, June 19, 1837.
26. Cole, p. 302.
27. Temin, p. 127.
28. Sellers, vol. 1, p. 162.
29. James Walker to Polk, March 14, 1836, Polk correspondence.
30. Sellers, vol. 1, p. 308.
31. Ibid., p. 334.
32. Ibid., p. 335.
33. *The Diary of James K. Polk*, September 13, 1845.
34. Ibid., October 14, 1847.

35. Ibid., December 27, 1847.
36. Ibid., January 4, 1848.
37. White, vol. 3, p. 272.
38. Sellers, vol. 1, p. 357.
39. White, vol. 3, p. 273.
40. Sellers records the victory margin at 2,462 (vol. 1, p. 373).
41. White, vol. 3, pp. 305–6.
42. Ibid.
43. Ibid., p. 20.
44. Sellers, vol. 1, p. 431.
45. Ibid., p. 434.

4. ANOTHER BARGAIN

1. Remini, *Clay*, p. 613.
2. Henry Clay to John Crittenden, June 3, 1842, Clay papers.
3. Sellers, vol. 1, p. 466.
4. Remini, *Andrew Jackson*, vol. 2, p. 218.
5. Aaron V. Brown to Polk, February 2, 1844, Polk correspondence.
6. Polk to Sackfield Maclin, January 17, 1842, Polk correspondence.
7. Aaron V. Brown to Polk, February 28, 1844, Polk correspondence.
8. Polk to Theophilus Fisk, March 20, 1844, Polk correspondence.
9. Chitwood, p. 343.
10. Remini, *Clay*, p. 641.
11. McCormac, p. 227, n. 44.
12. Cave Johnson to Polk, May 12, 1844, Polk correspondence.
13. Remini, *Andrew Jackson*, vol. 3, p. 498.
14. Seager, p. 208.
15. Polk to Cave Johnson, May 14, 1844, Polk correspondence.
16. Polk to Cave Johnson, May 13, 1844, Polk correspondence.
17. Ibid.
18. Polk to Cave Johnson, May 14, 1844, Polk correspondence.
19. Ibid.
20. Sellers, vol. 2, p. 96.
21. Ibid., p. 97.

22. Remini, *Clay*, p. 647.
23. Sellers, vol. 1, p. 186.
24. Ibid., p. 107.
25. Remini, *Andrew Jackson and His Indian Wars*, p. 228.
26. Polk to William R. Rucker, February 22, 1836, Polk correspondence.
27. Sellers, vol. 1, p. 312.
28. Ibid., p. 118.
29. Robert J. Walker to Polk, May 30, 1844, Polk correspondence.
30. Andrew J. Donelson to Polk, May 31, 1844, Polk correspondence.
31. Cave Johnson to Polk, June 1, 1844, Polk correspondence.
32. Cave Johnson to Polk, June 2, 1844, Polk correspondence.
33. Sellers, vol. 1, p. 119.
34. Polk to John K. Kane, June 8, 1844, n. 2, Polk correspondence.
35. Robert J. Walker to Polk, June 18, 1844, Polk correspondence.
36. Polk to John K. Kane, June 19, 1844, Polk correspondence.
37. Remini, *Clay*, pp. 650–51.
38. Ibid., pp. 656–57.
39. Sellers, vol. 2, p. 105.
40. Ibid., p. 140.
41. Polk to Henry Hubbard et al., June 12, 1844, Polk correspondence.
42. McCormac, p. 268.
43. Polk to Andrew J. Donelson, July 22, 1844, Polk correspondence.
44. McCormac, p. 269, n. 52, citing letter from Andrew Jackson to William B. Lewis, July 26, 1844.
45. Ibid., p. 271, citing letter from Andrew Jackson to Polk, July 23, 1844.
46. Sellers, vol. 2, p. 141.
47. Remini, *Clay*, p. 652, citing letter from Henry Clay to John Clayton, August 22, 1844.
48. Sellers, vol. 2, p. 141.
49. Ibid., vol. 1, pp. 64, 16.
50. J. G. M. Ramsey to Polk, July 10, 1844, Polk correspondence.
51. Sellers, vol. 2, p. 149.
52. Polk to Charles Ingersoll, October 4, 1844, Polk correspondence.

53. Remini, *Henry Clay,* pp. 659–60.
54. Ibid., p. 660.
55. Ibid., p. 666.
56. Ibid., p. 660.
57. Ibid., p. 662.
58. Ibid., p. 665.
59. Aaron V. Brown to Polk, January 25, 1845, Polk correspondence.
60. Sellers, vol. 2, p. 205.
61. Ibid., p. 219.

5. MEASURES OF A GREAT PRESIDENT

1. Sellers, vol. 2, p. 213.
2. Ridings and McIver, p. 78.
3. Sellers, vol. 2, p. 164.
4. Andrew Jackson to Polk, December 13, 1844, Polk correspondence.
5. Sellers, vol. 2, p. 200; Martin Van Buren to Polk, February 27, 1845, Polk correspondence.
6. *The Diary of James K. Polk,* July 7, 1847.
7. Remini, *Andrew Jackson,* vol. 2, p. 87, citing letter from Andrew Jackson to William B. Lewis, January 29, 1825.
8. Remini, *Andrew Jackson,* vol. 2, p. 88.
9. Birkner, p. 34, n. 25.
10. Aaron V. Brown to Polk, January 22, 1844, n. 3, Polk correspondence.
11. Loewen, p. 367; Remini, *Clay,* p. 586.
12. Klein, p. 32.
13. Birkner, p. 21.
14. Ibid.
15. Loewen, p. 367.
16. Sellers, vol. 2, p. 273, citing letter from Andrew Jackson to William B. Lewis, April 9, 1845.
17. Ibid., p. 277.
18. Ibid., citing letter from Polk to Andrew Jackson, March 26, 1845.
19. Ibid., p. 281, citing letter from Andrew Jackson to Francis Blair, April 9, 1845.

20. Polk inaugural address, p. 6.
21. Ibid., p. 7.
22. *The Diary of James K. Polk*, July 29, 1846.
23. Ibid., July 15, 1846.
24. Ibid., July 25, 1846.
25. Ibid., July 15, 1846.
26. Ibid., July 25, 1846.
27. Ibid., July 26, 1846.
28. Ibid., January 15, 1847.
29. Ibid., December 22, 1845.
30. Ibid., April 6, 1847.
31. Ibid., February 4, 1848.
32. Ibid., September 1, 1848.
33. Ibid., May 25, 1846.
34. Ibid., January 28, 1846.
35. Ibid.
36. Ibid., May 19, 1846.
37. Ibid., January 28, 1846.
38. Ibid., July 21, 1846.
39. Ibid., September 23, 1848.
40. Ibid., January 28, 1847.
41. Ibid., July 11, 1846.
42. Polk inaugural address, p. 9.
43. *The Diary of James K. Polk*, August 26, 1845.
44. Ibid., August 30, 1845.
45. Ibid., September 16, 1845.
46. Ibid., November 29, 1845.
47. Ibid., December 22, 1845.
48. Ibid., December 23, 1845.
49. Ibid., January 4, 1846.
50. Ibid., April 22, 1846.
51. Ibid., June 6, 1846.
52. Ibid.
53. Ibid., June 8, 1846.
54. Ibid., May 13, 1846.

55. Ibid., December 25, 1845.
56. Ibid., December 24, 1845.
57. McCoy, p. 220.

6. WAR

1. Bancroft, September 13, 1886.
2. Morison et al., p. 42.
3. *The Diary of James K. Polk*, January 7, 1847.
4. Sellers, vol. 2, p. 268.
5. *The Diary of James K. Polk*, November 21, 1846.
6. Ibid., February 20, 1847.
7. Nevins, p. 167, n. 9.
8. *The Diary of James K. Polk*, November 14, 1846.
9. Polk inaugural address, p. 7.
10. Bauer, p. 17.
11. Sellers, vol. 2, p. 262.
12. *The Diary of James K. Polk*, August 29, 1845.
13. Ibid., April 1, 1847.
14. Ibid., September 5, 1846.
15. Ibid., January 5, 1847.
16. Ibid., January 14, 1847.
17. Ibid., April 12, 1847.
18. Ibid., May 18, 1846.
19. Sellers, vol. 2, p. 441.
20. *The Diary of James K. Polk*, September 22, 1846.
21. Ibid., November 16, 1846.
22. Ibid., November 17, 1846.
23. Ibid., July 13, 1847.
24. Ibid., July 16, 1847.
25. Bauer, p. 11.
26. Ibid., p. 164.
27. Ibid., p. 194.
28. *The Diary of James K. Polk*, May 2, 1848.
29. Morison et al., p. 47.

30. Lincoln, p. 171.
31. Schlesinger, Jr., *Cycles*, p. 81.
32. Kennedy, p. 116.
33. *Journal of the House*, January 3, 1848, Library of Congress Web site.
34. De Voto, p. 135.
35. Lincoln, p. 167.
36. Ibid., p. 176.
37. Morison et al., p. 51.
38. Graebner, p. 216.
39. Ibid., p. 207.
40. Schlesinger, Jr., *Cycles*, p. 120.
41. Weinberg, p. 174.
42. Ibid., p. 177.
43. Ibid., p. 178.
44. Sellers, vol. 2, p. 481.
45. *The Diary of James K. Polk*, August 10, 1846.
46. Ibid., December 23, 1846.
47. Ibid.
48. Ibid., January 16, 1849.
49. Ibid.
50. Ibid.

7. POLK AT PEACE

1. *The Diary of James K. Polk*, June 15, 1847.
2. Ibid., November 8, 1848.
3. Ibid., February 24, 1849.
4. Ibid., February 27, 1849.
5. Ibid., March 25, 1849.
6. Ibid., April 2, 1849.
7. *Polk: The Diary of a President*, p. xi.
8. Haynes, pp. 72, 74.
9. Leonard, p. 43.
10. Byrnes, pp. 157–58.
11. McCoy, p. 53.

12. Remini, *Andrew Jackson*, vol. 3, p. 512.
13. De Voto, p. 7.
14. Bergeron, p. 135.
15. Bumgarner, p. 83.
16. McCormac, p. 250.
17. Sellers, vol. 1, p. 276.
18. Ibid., vol. 2, p. v.
19. *The Diary of James K. Polk*, September 8, 1846.
20. Ibid., July 16, 1846.
21. Schlesinger, Jr., *A Life*, p. 484.

Milestones

1795 James Knox Polk, first child of Samuel and Jane Knox Polk, born on Little Sugar Creek, Mecklenburg County, North Carolina. (Nov. 2)
   Infant Polk denied baptism by the Reverend James Wallis, a Presbyterian minister, after Samuel refuses to affirm Christian faith.

1803 Ezekiel Polk moves with most of his family to Tennessee; James stays in North Carolina with parents.
   Sarah Childress born at Murfreesboro, Tennessee. (Sept. 4)

1806 Samuel and Jane Polk bring family to middle Tennessee near Columbia, joining Ezekiel Polk and other Polk clan members.

1812 Dr. Ephraim McDowell removes urinary stones in major surgery performed at Danville, Kentucky.

1813 Attends Presbyterian academy at Mount Zion community near Columbia, Tennessee.

1814 Attends Bradley Academy in Murfreesboro. Finishes first in class. Classmate of Anderson Childress, brother of Sarah Childress.

1816 Admitted as sophomore student to University of North Carolina at Chapel Hill.

1818 Graduates first in class from University of North Carolina. Accepted to study law under Felix Grundy, Tennessee's premier lawyer.

1819 Named clerk of state senate meeting at state capital in Murfreesboro; courts Sarah Childress.

1820 Admitted to Tennessee bar; defends his father, charged with affray, fined one dollar.

1821 Joins state militia. Elected captain and later elevated to colonel.

1823 Elected to Tennessee House of Representatives; votes to nominate Andrew Jackson for president; votes to elect Jackson U.S. senator.

1824 Marries Sarah Childress on New Year's Day at Murfreesboro, Tennessee. (Jan. 1)

U.S. House of Representatives elects John Quincy Adams U.S. president. (Dec.)

1825 Henry Clay becomes secretary of state. He and President Adams charged with "corrupt bargain." (Mar. 5)

Elected to U.S. House of Representatives. (Aug. 5)

Takes oath as congressman. (Dec. 5)

1826 Makes first speech in Congress.

Argues for constitutional amendment denying House power to elect president.

Declares slavery "a common evil."

Signs note to help create pro-Jackson newspaper, the *United States Telegraph*, with Duff Green as editor.

1827 Reelected to House of Representatives over Andrew Erwin, leader of anti-Jackson faction in Tennessee. (Aug.)

Samuel Polk dies in Columbia. (Nov. 5)

Assigned to Committee on Foreign Affairs.

1828 Campaigns for Jackson for president in successful race against Adams.

Drafts answer to "Coffin Handbill."

1829 Elected to third term in House. (Aug.)

Remains on Foreign Affairs Committee.

Helps Jackson draft veto of Maysville road project; opposes and helps block House override of veto.

1831 Elected to fourth term in the House. (Aug.)

Remains on Foreign Affairs Committee.

1832 At President Jackson's request, named to Ways and Means Committee; investigates Bank of United States.

1833 Elected to fifth term in House. (Aug.)
      Chairs Ways and Means Committee; exposes Bank of United
      States corruption in floor speech.
1834 Loses to John Bell, fellow Tennessean, in election for Speaker
      of U.S. House. (June)
1835 Elected to sixth term in House. (Aug.)
      Defeats John Bell in election for House Speaker. (Dec. 7)
1836 Declares support for Martin Van Buren, who wins the presidency;
      opposes Tennessee senator Hugh Lawson White, who loses to Van
      Buren but carries state over Jackson-Polk political forces.
1837 Elected to seventh term. (Aug.)
      Reelected House Speaker. (Sept.)
1838 Declares candidacy for governor of Tennessee.
1839 Ends tenure in Congress; begins campaign for governor.
      (Mar.)
      Elected governor over incumbent Newt Cannon. (Aug.)
      Inaugurated governor. (Oct. 14)
      Nominated vice president by resolution of the Tennessee Leg-
      islature.
1840 Declares for reelection as governor. (July 4)
1841 Loses governor's race to James "Lean Jimmy" Jones. (Aug. 5)
1842 Martin Van Buren visits Jackson and Polk at Hermitage; and
      Polk at Columbia. (Apr./May)
      Van Buren visits Henry Clay at Lexington. (May)
1843 Loses governor's race to incumbent Governor Jones. (Aug. 3)
1844 Declares support for annexation of Texas. (Apr. 22)
      Van Buren and Clay both come out against annexation of
      Texas in separate newspaper statements. (Apr. 26)
      Henry Clay nominated Whig candidate at Baltimore. (May 1)
      President John Tyler nominated for election at Democratic-
      Republican convention at Baltimore. (May 27)
      Nominated for president at Democratic convention at Balti-
      more. Silas Wright of New York declines vice presidential
      nomination; George Dallas of Pennsylvania accepts; Polk
      called "Young Hickory" by Democratic press.
      Elected president. (Nov. 5)

1845   Helps Tyler get House and Senate approval of Texas treaty annexation resolution.

Names cabinet: James Buchanan, secretary of state; Robert Walker, secretary of the Treasury; William Marcy, secretary of war; George Bancroft, secretary of the navy; John Y. Mason, attorney general; Cave Johnson, postmaster general. (Mar. 6–10)

Mexican president Herrera ends diplomatic relations with United States (Mar. 28)

Terminates Democratic party relationship with Francis Blair and his *Globe.* Brings in Thomas Ritchie of the *Richmond Enquirer* as editor of new party paper, the *Washington Union.* (Apr.)

Andrew Jackson dies at Hermitage. Last letter warned Polk of Treasury Department corruption. (June 8)

Directs General Zachary Taylor to station troops on northern border of Rio Grande near Matamoras. (June 15)

Decides to record daily events in diary. (Aug. 26)

Commissions John Slidell minister to Mexico. (Sept. 16)

Present at opening of U.S. Naval Academy. (Oct. 10)

Rejects British proposal to set dispute over Oregon boundary at forty-ninth parallel. (Dec. 27)

Texas becomes twenty-eighth state of Union. (Dec. 29)

1846   Constitutional Treasury Bill passed by the House of Representatives. (April 2)

Mexican army ambushes Taylor's troops north of Rio Grande, U.S. soldiers killed, others captured. (Apr. 24)

Taylor wins battles at Palo Alto and Resaca de la Palma; Polk learns of Mexican attack of Apr. 24. (May 8–9)

War against Mexico declared by Congress. (May 13)

Removes General Scott from command. (May 25)

Cabinet votes to send treaty proposal with British on Oregon boundary to Senate; Polk signs the treaty. Boundary set at forty-ninth parallel. First of four "great measures" achieved. (June 15)

Signs bill reducing tariff. Second great measure achieved. (July 30)

Signs Constitutional Treasury bill. Third great measure achieved. (Aug.)

Vetoes bill to provide internal improvements through Rivers and Harbors Act. (Aug. 3)

1847 General Taylor, outnumbered four to one, wins Battle of Buena Vista. (Feb. 23)

General Scott takes Veracruz. (Mar. 29)

Designates Nicholas Trist to negotiate peace with Mexico. (Apr. 10)

Attends groundbreaking of Smithsonian. (May 1)

General Scott takes Mexico City. (Sept. 14)

Dismisses Nicholas Trist from authorized negotiations with the Mexicans; Trist continues to negotiate. (Oct. 25)

Vetoes Wisconsin Internal Improvements Act. (Dec. 15)

1848 Discovery of gold in California. (Jan. 24)

Mexican war ends with signing of treaty. (Feb. 2)

Southwest territories become part of Union; fourth "great measure" achieved.

Attends groundbreaking for Washington Monument. (July 4)

General Taylor, the Whig candidate, defeats Lewis Cass, the Democratic candidate, for president. Van Buren, Free Soil candidate, runs third. (Nov. 7)

1849 Department of Interior law signed. Spends last night as president prepared to veto any last-minute internal improvement act passed by Congress; none is passed. (Mar. 3)

President Taylor inaugurated. (Mar. 4)

Begins monthlong journey home to Tennessee. (Mar. 6)

Visits mother, Jane, at Columbia. (Apr. 5)

Baptized by Methodist minister. (June)

Dies; remains placed in a temporary vault at the Nashville city cemetery while the official tomb at Polk Place is constructed. (June 15)

1850 Remains transferred to the tomb at Polk Place. (May 22)

1852 Jane Knox Polk (mother) dies.

1891 Sarah Childress Polk (wife) dies.

1893 Remains removed from Polk Place tomb to the grounds of the Tennessee state Capitol.

ABOUT THE AUTHOR

John Seigenthaler is the founder of the First Amendment Center at Vanderbilt University. An administrative assistant to Robert F. Kennedy, he was an award-winning journalist for *The Nashville Tennessean* for forty-three years, finally serving as the paper's editor, publisher, and CEO, and was named founding editorial director of *USA Today* in 1982. He lives in Nashville, Tennessee

Selected Bibliography

Bancroft, George. "Notes on a Sketch of James K. Polk" (typescript). George Bancroft Collection. New York Public Library, 1886.

Barber, J. *The Presidential Character.* New York: Prentice-Hall, Inc., 1972.

Bauer, K. Jack. *The Mexican War, 1846–1848.* Lincoln: University of Nebraska Press, 1974.

Bergeron, Paul H. *The Presidency of James K. Polk.* Lawrence: University Press of Kansas, 1987.

Birkner, Michael J., ed. *James Buchanan and the Political Crisis of the 1850s.* Selinsgrove, Penn.: Susquehanna University Press, 1996.

Bumgarner, John R. *Sarah Childress Polk: A Biography of the Remarkable First Lady.* Jefferson, N.C.: McFarland, 1997.

Byrnes, Mark Eaton. *James K. Polk.* Santa Barbara, Calif.: ABC-CLIO, 2001.

Chitwood, Oliver Perry. *John Tyler: Champion of the Old South.* New York: D. Appleton-Century, 1939.

Clay, Henry. Papers. Vols. 1–10. Louisville: University of Kentucky Press, 1959– .

Cole, Donald B. *Martin Van Buren and the American Political System.* Princeton: Princeton University Press, 1984.

DeFiore, Jane Crumpler. "Sarah Childress Polk." In Carroll Van West, ed., *Tennessee Encyclopedia of History and Culture.* Nashville: Tennessee Historical Society, 1998.

De Voto, Bernard Augustine. *The Year of Decision: 1846.* New York: St. Martin's Press, 2000.

Goodstein, Anita S. "Slavery." In Carroll Van West, ed., *Tennessee Encyclopedia of History and Culture.* Nashville: Tennessee Historical Society, 1998.

Graebner, Norman A., ed. *Manifest Destiny.* Indianapolis: Bobbs-Merrill, 1968.

Guild, Jo. C. *Old Times in Tennessee.* Nashville: Travel, Eastman & Howell, 1878.

Harris, J. George. *Polk Campaign Biography.* Knoxville: Tennessee Presidents Trust, 1990.

Haynes, Sam W. *James K. Polk and the Expansionist Impulse.* New York: Longman, 1997.

Ikard, Robert W. "Surgical Operation on James K. Polk by Ephraim McDowell or the Search for Polk's Gallstones." *Tennessee Quarterly* 43, no. 2 (1984): 121–31.

Jenkins, John S. *James Knox Polk, and a History of His Administration: Embracing the Annexation of Texas, the Difficulties with Mexico, the Settlement of the Oregon Question, and Other Important Events.* Buffalo, N.Y.: J. E. Beardsley, 1850.

Kennedy, Robert F. *Just Friends and Brave Enemies.* New York: Harper & Row, 1962.

Klein, Philip Shriver. *President James Buchanan.* University Park: Pennsylvania State University Press, 1962.

Leckie, Robert. *From Sea to Shining Sea: From the War of 1812 to the Mexican War, the Saga of America's Expansion.* New York: HarperCollins, 1993.

Leonard, Thomas M. *James K. Polk—a Clear and Unquestionable Destiny.* Wilmington, Del.: Scholarly Resources Books, 2001.

Lincoln, Abraham. *Speeches and Writings, 1832–1858.* New York: Literary Classics of the United States (Viking Press), 1989.

Loewen, James W. *Lies Across America: What Our Historic Sites Get Wrong.* New York: New Press, 1999.

Lomask, Milton. *This Slender Reed: A Life of James K. Polk.* New York: Farrar, Straus & Giroux, 1966.

McCormac, Eugene Irving. *James K. Polk: A Political Biography.* Berkeley: University of California Press, 1922.

McCoy, Charles Allan. *Polk and the Presidency.* Austin: University of Texas Press, 1960.

Meyers, Jeffrey, ed. *The Biographer's Art: New Essays.* New York: New Amsterdam, 1989.

Morison, Samuel Eliot, Frederick Merk, and Frank Freidel. *Dissent in Three American Wars.* Cambridge: Harvard University Press, 1970.

Morrel, Martha McBride. *"Young Hickory," the Life and Times of President James K. Polk.* New York: E. P. Dutton, 1949.

Nelson, Anson, and Fanny Nelson. *Memorials of Sarah Childress Polk.* New York: A. D. F. Randolph, 1892.

Parks, Joseph Howard. *Felix Grundy: Champion of Democracy.* Baton Rouge: Louisiana State University Press, 1940.

Peterson, Norma Lois. *The Presidencies of William Henry Harrison and John Tyler.* Lawrence: University Press of Kansas, 1989.

Polk, James K. Correspondence. Ed. Herbert Weaver. Vol. 1, 1817–1832. Nashville: Vanderbilt University Press, 1969.

———. Correspondence. Ed. Herbert Weaver. Vol. 2, 1833–1834. Nashville: Vanderbilt University Press, 1972.

———. Correspondence. Ed. Herbert Weaver. Vol. 3, 1835–1836. Nashville: Vanderbilt University Press, 1975.

———. Correspondence. Ed. Herbert Weaver. Vol. 4, 1837–1838. Nashville: Vanderbilt University Press, 1977.

———. Correspondence. Ed. Wayne Cutler. Vol. 5, 1839–1841. Nashville: Vanderbilt University Press, 1979.

———. Correspondence. Ed. Wayne Cutler. Vol. 6, 1842–1843. Nashville: Vanderbilt University Press, 1983.

———. Correspondence. Ed. Wayne Cutler. Vol. 7, January–August 1844. Nashville: Vanderbilt University Press, 1989.

———. Correspondence. Ed. Wayne Cutler. Vol. 8, September–December 1844. Nashville: Vanderbilt University Press, 1993.

———. Correspondence. Ed. Wayne Cutler. Vol. 9, January–June 1845. Nashville: Vanderbilt University Press, 1996.

————. *The Diary of James K. Polk.* Ed. Milo Milton Quaife. Vols. 1–4. Chicago: A. C. McClurg, 1910.

————. Inaugural address. Ed. R. G. Hall. Knoxville: Tennessee Presidents Trust, 1993.

————. *Polk: The Diary of a President—1845–1849, Covering the Mexican War, the Acquisition of Oregon, and the Conquest of California and the Southwest.* Ed. Allan Nevins. New York: Longmans, Green, 1929.

Polk, William R. *Polk's Folly: An American Family History.* New York: Doubleday, 2000.

Reedy, George E. *Twilight of the Presidency.* New York: World Publishing, 1970.

Remini, Robert V. *Andrew Jackson and the Course of American Empire.* Vol. 1, 1767–1821. New York: Harper & Row, 1977.

————. *Andrew Jackson and the Course of American Freedom.* Vol. 2, 1822–1832. New York: Harper & Row, 1981.

————. *Andrew Jackson and the Course of American Democracy.* Vol. 3, 1833–1845. New York: Harper & Row, 1984.

————. *Andrew Jackson and His Indian Wars.* New York: Viking Press, 2001.

————. *The Election of Andrew Jackson.* Philadelphia: J. B. Lippincott, 1963.

————. *Henry Clay: Statesman for the Union.* New York: W. W. Norton, 1991.

Ridings, William J., Jr., and Stuart B. McIver. *Rating the Presidents: A Ranking of U.S. Leaders, from the Great and Honorable to the Dishonest and Incompetent.* Secaucus, N.J.: Carol Publishing Group, 1997.

Schlesinger, Arthur M., Jr. *The Age of Jackson.* Boston: Little, Brown, 1945.

————. *The Cycles of American History.* Boston: Houghton Mifflin, 1999.

————. *The Imperial Presidency.* Boston: Houghton Mifflin, 1973.

————. *A Life in the Twentieth Century.* Boston: Houghton Mifflin, 2000.

————. "Rating the Presidents: Washington to Clinton." *Political Science Quarterly* 112, no. 3 (1997): 179–90.

Seager, Robert, II. *And Tyler Too: A Biography of John and Julia Gardiner Tyler.* Norwalk, Conn.: Easton Press, 1963.

Sellers, Charles Grier. *James K. Polk.* Vol. 1, *The Jacksonian* (1795–1843). Princeton: Princeton University Press, 1957.

———. *James K. Polk.* Vol. 2, *The Continentalist* (1843–1846). Princeton: Princeton University Press, 1966.

Temin, Peter. *The Jacksonian Economy.* New York: W. W. Norton, 1969.

Tocqueville, Alexis de. *Democracy in America,* 2 vols. New York: Vintage Books, 1945.

Walker, Jane C. *John Tyler: A President of Many Firsts.* Blacksburg, Va.: McDonald Woodward Publishing, 2001.

Weinberg, Albert K. *Manifest Destiny: A Study of Nationalist Expansionism in American History.* Baltimore: Johns Hopkins Press, 1935.

West, Carroll Van, ed. *Voices for Union.* Nashville: Rutledge Hill Press, 1998.

White, Robert Hiram. *Messages of the Governors of Tennessee.* Vols. 1–3. Nashville: Tennessee Historical Commission, 1952.

Wooldridge, John, ed. *History of Nashville, Tennessee.* Nashville: Charles Elder Bookseller, 1890.

Acknowledgments

In the research and writing of *James K. Polk* I drew on the knowledge and expertise of many people, including earlier Polk biographers and historians, to formulate my perceptions of our eleventh president. I alone, of course, am responsible for the depiction here. My evaluation of Polk was most heavily influenced by his own words—preserved in his extraordinary presidential diary and his extensive correspondence.

My thanks to Arthur Schlesinger, whose friendly and insightful guidance went beyond anything expected or required of the general editor of this series of presidential biographies. His attention to historical detail and his intuitive recommendations made my manuscript not only manageable but more readable.

Robin Dennis of Times Books applied her gifted editing skills and further contributed to the book's cogency and lucidity. Others at Times Books to whom I am indebted include Chris O'Connell and David Sobel. My thanks also to Vicki Haire for her sharp copyediting.

I am particularly grateful to Wayne Cutler, director of the Polk papers project at the University of Tennessee, for hours of discerning conversation and good advice. He and his staff were unfailingly accessible and helpful.

To Madison Gray, a special word of appreciation for her tireless efforts in researching, fact-checking, and coordinating needed revisions.

Others to whom I am indebted in diverse ways each will understand include: Frank Boehm, Bernard Brody, Amon Carter Evans, William Ewers, Dick Fulton, Edwin Gleaves, Doris Kearns Goodwin, Charles Haynes, John Holtzapple, Robert Ikard, Dean Knoll, Charles Overby, Ken Paulson, William Polk, Robert Remini, Tom Seigenthaler, John Sergent, Jean Kennedy Smith, Tiffany Villager, Tammy Wheeler, Laurie Woods, the staff of the special archive collection of the New York Public Library, the staff of the Jean and Alexander Heard Central Library at Vanderbilt University, the staff of the Tennessee State Library and Archives, and the staff of the James K. Polk Ancestral Home Polk House in Columbia, Tennessee.

Finally, words cannot adequately express my enduring gratitude to Dolores Watson Seigenthaler who, for too many months, was married to the contentious ghost of James K. Polk as well as to me.

Index

Aberdeen, Lord, 125, 127
abolition/abolitionists, 57, 77, 80,
    86–87, 85, 99, 119, 150
Adams, John, 11
Adams, John Quincy, 5–6, 33, 35,
    36, 37, 38, 39, 53, 56, 67, 78,
    108, 145
    defeated in election, 41–42,
      43
    efforts to reelect, 40
    signed tariff bill, 88
Adams administration, 39, 57
Alamo, 8, 76, 135, 144
"All Mexico" movement, 147
American System, 35, 43, 79
anticipatory self-defense, 146
Atocha, A. J., 143–44

Baltimore conventions, 3, 7, 8, 9,
    78–85
Bancroft, George, 11, 18, 19,
    82–83, 84, 102, 103, 131
    secretary of navy, 105, 106,
      140–41
bank notes, 57, 58
Bank of the United States, 44, 55,
    122
bank war, 48–53, 57–58
banking lobby, 31–32, 34, 66
banking policy, 31–32

banks, 29, 30–31, 33, 48–49, 59
Barber, James David, 2
Battle of New Orleans, 28
Battle of San Jacinto, 76, 135,
    136
Bauer, K. Jack, 140, 141–42
Bell, John, 39, 50, 57, 59, 60, 61,
    62, 63
    Polk's battle with, 53–56
Benton, Thomas Hart, 27, 58, 74,
    92, 104, 134
    Polk lost as friend, 142–43
    and Texas annexation issue, 100,
      101
Bergeron, Paul H., 154
Biddle, Nicholas, 31, 48–53, 54,
    55, 58, 59, 60, 62
Bigelow Papers (Lowell), 145
Birney, James G., 99
Blair, Francis, 7, 45, 51, 93–94,
    101, 105, 112
Blount, William, 17, 28, 30
Britain/British, 14, 20, 103,
    128
    acquiring Oregon from, 102–3,
      104, 123–27, 131
    war with, 28
Brown, Aaron, 73, 74–75, 81, 99,
    100, 104, 109, 111, 112, 115,
    137, 153

Buchanan, James, 74, 83, 85, 92, 104, 116, 156
  All Mexico movement, 147
  and Mexican war, 139
  and Oregon issue, 123–24, 126, 127–28
  patronage, 133
  Polk's confrontations with, 121
  relationship with Polk, 128–30
  secretary of state, 107–11, 121, 147, 151, 153
  sexual preference, 109–11
  and Supreme Court, 129–30
Buena Vista, 134, 137, 147
Buffalo-to-New Orleans road, 35, 45–46
Bumgarner, John Reed, 154
Bush, George W., 146
Butler, Benjamin, 82, 84, 85, 93, 99, 106, 107, 119
Byrnes, Mark E., 154

cabinet (Polk), 104–8, 111, 126, 127, 128, 129, 133, 139, 142, 153
Calhoun, John C., 39, 54, 74, 75, 83, 92, 104, 119–20
  Jackson's break with, 45
  nullifiers and, 64, 99
  and Oregon issue, 126, 127
  secretary of state, 90, 93, 100, 104, 105, 132
  and slavery issue, 85
  and tariff, 47–48, 116
  and Texas annexation, 100, 104
  theory of nullification, 88
  and Wilmot Proviso, 148, 149, 150
California, Polk's goal to acquire from Mexico, 1, 103, 104, 128, 131–33, 140–43, 147, 152
Cambreleng, Churchill, 57, 107
Cameron, Simon, 119–20
Cannon, Newton, 64–65, 68
career (Polk), 2, 3–4, 7–9
  clerk and lawyer, 22–26, 30–31

  governor of Tennessee, 3, 61, 64–69, 74
  in House, 6, 36–42, 43, 89
  in politics, 25, 27, 29, 30–31, 34, 35
  Speaker of the House, 3, 54, 56–60, 61–63, 64, 83, 87, 114, 148
  state legislator, 5
  see also presidency (Polk)
Carroll, William, 30–31, 32, 34, 43, 64
Cass, Lewis, 73, 74, 82, 83, 84, 92, 104, 127, 153
"Civil Disobedience" (Thoreau), 145
Clay, Henry, 4–6, 8, 9, 12, 35, 36, 37, 38, 39, 41, 49, 55, 56, 62, 64
  attack on Jackson's image, 40
  calling at White House, 117–18
  candidacy, 33, 47, 52, 79
  and internal improvements, 46–47
  lost elections, 52, 97–99
  met with Van Buren, 70–72
  mocking Buchanan, 110
  and national bank, 61
  presidential campaign, 91–92, 94, 95, 96, 97
  scheme to enlarge federal power, 43
  secretary of state, 108
  and slavery issue, 77, 85
  and tariffs, 88, 89, 90, 114
  and Texas annexation issue, 71–72, 76–77, 78, 79
  and Whig party, 119
"Coffin Handbill," 40
commander in chief (Polk), 132, 134–35, 138, 139
Congress, 61, 49, 131
  and Oregon issue, 126, 127
  Polk in/and, 33–42, 122
  war over issues, 45–47
  and war with Mexico, 132–33, 136, 140, 148
  and Wilmot Proviso, 148, 149

Conscience Whigs, 131–32, 145
Constitution, 36–38
Constitutional Treasury, 131
Constitutional Treasury Act, 102,
    122
Cook, D. P., 36–37, 38
Cook, Edward, 10
"corrupt bargain," 5, 6, 33–34, 35,
    37, 92, 108
corruption, 37, 43, 49, 50, 51
Crawford, William H., 5, 32, 33
credit economy, 49, 57

Dallas, George, 85, 88, 89, 94,
    107, 108
  vice president, 115–16, 133,
    147
"dark horse" candidate, 80, 90–97
Democracy, the, 4, 7, 10, 68
Democratic party/Democrats, 7,
    71, 76, 81, 85, 113
  conventions, 68, 78–85
  factionalism, 107–8
  in House, 56, 57, 60
  joining Whigs on votes, 119–20
  lost House, 116, 144
  schisms, 105
  Tennessee, 66, 68, 74
Democratic-Republican party, 36,
    79
depression, 24, 29, 31
De Voto, Bernard, 146, 154
Dialectic Society, 22, 24
diary (Polk), 13–14, 16, 18, 101,
    115, 119–21, 122, 123, 128,
    129, 133, 134, 137, 140, 144,
    153–54, 155, 156
Dickinson, Daniel, 114, 147
Donelson, Andrew Jackson, 80, 81
Donelson, Jack, 89, 94

Eaton, John, 33, 38, 39, 43
  scandal, 44–45
Eaton, Margaret O'Neale
    Timberlake (Peggy), 43,
    44–45
economic justice, 6, 29, 113, 122

economy (the), 52, 57–60, 64, 79
education, upgrading, 65, 66
Elias (slave boy), 26, 86
Emancipator, The, 150
Emerson, Ralph Waldo, 145
Engels, Friedrich, 147
Erwin, Andrew, 28–29, 30, 32,
    34–35, 42
Everett, Edward, 37–38
expansionism, 6, 15, 147

factionalism, 107, 108
federal funds
  in pet banks, 51, 52, 57–58
  in private banks, 102, 122
  in Second Bank of the United
    States, 49
  independent Treasury for, 60
  in state banks, 61
Federal Revenue System, 122
federalism, 11, 29, 36, 37
Federalist party, 36, 119
"Fifty-four forty or fight," 123, 124
First Bank of the United States,
    49
fiscal policy, 49
fiscal politics, 29–32
Florida, 28, 45
Force Bill, 48
Frémont, John C., 141–43

gold, discovery of, 143
gold and silver (specie), 23, 29, 31,
    32, 49, 58, 59
Goliad, 8, 76, 135
government, 11–12, 29, 35, 37
government land, 58
Green, Duff, 39, 45, 56, 93
Grundy, Felix, 23, 24, 31, 32, 54,
    60, 66, 153, 155

Hamilton, Alexander, 11, 12, 22,
    29, 49, 113
Harris, J. George, 19–20
Harrison, William Henry, 4, 55,
    56
Haynes, Sam W., 154

Haywood, William, 22, 115–16
Hermitage, 3, 31, 33, 60, 65, 70, 72, 80, 104, 111
Herrera, José Joaquin de, 125, 126, 135–36, 143
homosexuality, 111
House of Representatives, 5, 36, 56
  disorder in, 61–63
  Polk in, 6, 36–42, 43, 89
  Polk Speaker of, 3, 54, 56–60, 61–63, 64, 83, 87, 114, 148
  Ways and Means Committee, 50, 51, 57
Houston, Sam, 40, 61–62, 76, 94, 100, 125, 135
  and All Mexico movement, 147
  won Texas revolution, 136

independent treasury
  goal of Polk's presidency, 102, 121–22, 131
Independent Treasury Act, 60, 121–22
inflation, 58, 59
Ingersoll, Charles J., 89–90
internal improvements, 34–36, 79
  Jackson opposed, 44, 45–46
  Polk and, 45–47
  state, 65, 66
  tariff and, 88

Jackson, Andrew (Old Hickory), 1–2, 3–5, 6, 7, 8, 9, 25, 36, 110, 111
  attacks on, 5, 40
  bank war, 48–53
  bigamy and adultery charge, 5, 41
  break with Calhoun, 45
  and Buchanan, 108–9
  cabinet, 105, 106
  candidacy, 34, 37–39, 40–42
  conflicts, 27
  elected president, 41–42, 43, 52
  governor of Florida, 30, 31
  heir to Jeffersonian philosophy, 12

and independent Treasury, 60
mentor to Polk, 2, 3
nullification issue, 47, 48
philosophy, 113–14
and Polk, 27–42, 53–54, 60, 63, 64, 65
and Polk appointments, 105, 111–12
and Polk's campaign for president, 80, 81, 92, 93–94, 99
Polk's debt to, 104
Polk's support for, 89
president, 31–32, 44, 45, 47, 48
presidential campaigns, 23, 28, 32–33, 34
ranking as great president, 103
and slavery issue, 85, 86, 149
"Specie Circular," 58, 59
and Texs annexation issue, 78
Van Buren met with, 70, 72–73
war hero, 28, 29
Jackson, Rachel Donelson Robards, 5, 28, 41
Jackson administration
  cabinet debacle in, 104
  Polk defender of, 43–69
Jacksonian Democracy, 6, 64, 69
  rebuilding, 104–11
Jacksonian Democrats, 3, 11, 34
Jarnagin, Spencer, 115
Jefferson, Thomas, 1–2, 6, 11, 13, 16, 22, 29, 34, 64
  cabinet, 105
  election, 36
  on Jackson, 27
  legacy of, 113
  philosophy, 12
  ranking as great president, 103
Jeffersonian republicanism, 11, 28
Jenkins, John, 24, 34
Johnson, Andrew, 83, 121
Johnson, Cave, 54, 60, 62, 75, 78, 104, 112, 137
  and Baltimore convention, 80–82, 83, 84
  and Mexican war, 139

Johnson, Cave (*cont'd*)
    and Polk prospects to run for
        vice-president, 73
    and Polk's presidential
        campaign, 92
    postmaster general, 105, 115
    and tariff issue, 89
Johnson, Lyndon, 118, 146
Johnson, Richard M., 64, 68, 73,
    74
Jones, James C. ("Lean Jimmy"),
    67, 68

Kane, John, 89, 90, 113
Kearney, Stephen W., 140,
    141–42, 144, 147, 148
Kennedy, John F., 118, 154
Kennedy, Robert, 145–46
King, William Rufus, 73, 74, 75
    Buchanan and, 109–10

Land Grab Act, 17
Leonard, Thomas M., 154
Lewis, William B., 32, 33, 38, 39,
    53, 94
    in Jackson administration, 43
    Polk cut out of office, 112
Lincoln, Abraham, 2, 144, 145,
    146, 147, 148, 150
Loco Focos, 56, 59
"Log Cabin and Hard Cider"
    campaign, 91
Lowell, James Russell, 145

McCalla, William L., 16
McCormac, Eugene, 11, 38,
    154–55
McCoy, Charles A., 130, 154
McDuffie, George, 36–37, 38
Madison, James, 6, 13, 28
Madisonian (newspaper), 59
Manifest Destiny, 103, 122–28,
    147
manumission, 150
Marcy, William, 107, 108, 136
    and Mexican war, 138, 139
    patronage, 133

Marx, Karl, 147
Mason, John Y., 22, 75, 105, 139
Maysville road, 46
Mecklenburg Resolves, 17
Memphis Enquirer, 65
Merk, Frederick, 116, 144
Mexican Congress, 125, 136
Mexican war, 135–41
    agreement ending, 151–52
    diplomatic initiatives to end,
        143–47
    protest against, 144–46, 147,
        152
    support for, 146–47
Mexico, 124, 125–26, 148
    acquiring California from, 103,
        104
    relations with, 125–26, 135–36,
        141
    war with, 1, 14, 15–16, 116,
        128, 132, 134
    war with: Polk's generals in,
        133–38
Mexico City, 139, 140, 144, 147,
    151
Monroe, James, 6, 27, 28, 45
Monterey, 141
Monterrey, 134, 137, 139, 140
Mormons, 15
mudslinging, 94–95

Nashville Central Committee, 40,
    41
Nashville-to-Columbia toll road,
    34
Nashville Union, 19, 65
national bank, 6, 54, 61, 79
National Banner, 51
National Intelligencer, 51, 61, 76
National Republicans, 47
Nevins, Allan, 154
New Mexico, 1, 131, 147, 152
New York (state), 92, 99, 106
Nicholson, A. O. P., 66*n*, 68, 74
North (the)
    and tarifs, 87, 88, 90, 113, 114
Northwest, 103, 122, 124

nullification, 44, 56, 104, 116
    politics of, 47–48
    theory of, 88
nullifiers, 54, 56, 64, 67, 80, 99
    and abolition, 87
    and tariff, 90

Oregon, Polk's goal to acquire,
    102–3, 104, 116, 122–28
Oregon Territory, 1, 15, 85, 128
Overton, John, 28, 30, 32, 33, 38,
    40, 41
Overton-Blount faction, 30, 32

Pakenham, Richard, 123, 124, 125
Panic of 1819, 23, 29
Panic of 1837, 57, 58–59
paper notes, 23, 29, 30, 49, 59
Paredes y Arrillaga, Mariano, 126,
    143
Paris West Tennessean, 65
Parrott, William, 125, 135–36
partisanship, 10, 67, 68, 69,
    133–34
patronage, 37, 38, 46, 50
    Polk and, 114–15, 121, 132–33,
    134
Peel, Sir Robert, 123, 125, 127
Pennsylvania, 88, 92, 133
pet banks, 51, 52, 57–58, 59, 60,
    122
Peyton, Ann, 39, 40
Peyton, Bailie, 62–63
Pierce, Franklin, 110, 135
Pillow, Gideon, 81, 82–83, 84, 90,
    151–52
    military appointment, 134
politics
    in bank war, 52–53
    fiscal, 29–32
    of nullification, 47–48
    Polk in/and, 25, 27, 29, 30–31,
    34, 35
    of slavery, 85–87
    of Washington, 36, 38
Polk, Ezekiel, 11, 12–13, 16,
    17–18, 95–96

Polk, James Knox
    achievements, 1–3, 156
    ambition to be president,
    63–64
    authorized campaign biography,
    19–20
    battles with Bell, 53–56
    character traits, 10
    death of, 15, 150
    early life, 10–12, 13, 18–22
    education, 11, 13, 19, 20–22
    ego, 121
    friends/friendship, 23, 82, 137,
    153
    head of own administration,
    111–12
    health/illness, 11, 18, 153–54
    health/illness: surgery, 19–20
    legacy of, 152–56
    micromanager, 64, 103
    military title, 25
    nickname "Young Hickory," 4, 92
    personal characteristics, 1, 22,
    63, 96, 103, 119, 121, 133,
    154–55, 156
    political enemies, 16, 119
    political indoctrination, 11, 12
    religious life, 12–16, 21
    reputation, 95
    sense of propriety, 120
    standing among presidents, 10,
    103, 154–56
    youngest president, 93, 103–4
    see also career (Polk); presidency
    (Polk); vice presidency
Polk, Jane Knox, 12, 13, 16, 18, 25
Polk, Samuel, 11, 12, 13, 16,
    18–19, 24, 25, 31, 95
    commercial interests, 21
    owned slaves, 85–86
Polk, Sarah Childress, 25–26, 44,
    85, 98, 99, 100, 103, 109,
    111, 153
    as first lady, 116–18
    Polk attended church with,
    13–14, 95, 142, 155
    slaves left to, 150

Polk, Thomas, 17
Polk, William, 24, 25, 38
Polk administration
    greatness of, 156
    war defining, 131–33
Polks (the), 17–18
presidency, 6
    Clay and Van Buren courted, 71
    Jackson and, 28
presidency (Polk), 3, 8–9, 48, 70,
    71, 80–82, 83–85, 87, 97–99
    dark horse campaign, 90–97
    election, 8–9, 97–99
    "great measures," 102–30, 131
    one-term, 92–93
Presidential Character, The
    (Barber), 2
presidential elections, 6, 7, 8–9,
    36–38, 52, 56, 97–99
presidential greatness, 1–2,
    102–30, 154
press, 40–41, 45, 49, 112
    Whig, 65
Princeton (steamship), 75
private banks, 1, 102, 122
public opinion
    regarding annexation of Texas,
    8–9, 71, 76–77
public works projects, 34–36

Ramsey, J. M. G., 95, 96
recession, 52, 66
Regency, 98, 99, 107
religion, 12–16, 21
religionists, 67
Remini, Robert, 52, 71n, 76, 86,
    98, 108, 110, 154
Republic of Texas, 77, 144
    annexation of, 8–9
    opposition to annexation of,
    70–72
Republican doctrine
    Polk and, 2, 11
republicanism, 22, 29, 36
    Jeffersonian, 11, 28
Republicans, 34
Rio Grande, 136, 147

Ritchie, Thomas, 112
Roman Catholics, 15–16
Roorbach Fraud, 96–97
Roosevelt, Franklin, 19
Roosevelt, Theodore, 154

Santa Anna, Antonio López de,
    136, 143–44, 148, 151
Schlesinger, Arthur, Jr., 156
Schlesinger, Arthur, Sr., 154
Scott, Winfield, 133–35, 138–40,
    144, 147, 148, 151–52
secession, 47, 48, 88
Second Bank of the United States,
    31, 32, 48–53
secretary of state, 6, 93
    Buchanan, 107–11, 121, 147,
    151, 153
    Calhoun, 90, 93, 100, 104, 105,
    132
    Polk cabinet, 106, 107–8
    Polk his own, 104, 130
Sedition Act, 11
Sellers, Charles, 12n, 67, 101, 155
Semple, James, 15, 114–16
Senate, 33
    Texas annexation issue in, 100,
    101
separation of church and state, 13,
    16
slave states, 72, 75, 76
slavery/slaves, 29, 75, 132
    Clay and, 96–98
    outlawed, 150
    politics of, 85–87
    Polk and, 96–97, 150
    states deciding, 77, 78
slavery issue, 57, 72, 77–78
    Polk and, 77–78, 85–87, 149–50
    in territory acquired from
    Mexico, 148–50
Slidell, John, 89, 125–26
South (the), 97
    and tariffs, 87, 88, 90
South Carolina, 47, 58, 92
specie
    see gold and silver (specie)

"Specie Circular," 58, 59–60
speculation, 58
state banks, 59, 65, 66
State Department, 104, 106
states' rights, 46, 47, 149
Stevenson, Andrew, 53, 54
Stockton, Robert, 141–42

Taney, Roger, 52
tariff(s), 1, 47, 67, 79, 87–90
   Jackson and, 6, 44, 48
   Polk and, 88–90
   Polk's goal to lower, 102,
      113–16, 122, 131
Tariff of Abominations, 47, 88
taxing policy, 113–14
Taylor, Zachary, 125, 133–35,
      136–38, 140, 144, 147, 148,
      152
   candidate for president, 135,
      138
   elected president, 153
Temin, Peter, 59
Tennessee, 1, 18, 42, 50, 72
   banking reform, 31–32
   in depression, 29–30
   Jackson's political control of, 55,
      56
   Polk governor of, 3, 61, 64–69,
      74
   Polk lost, 7–8, 99
   Polk's program for, 65–66
   Whiggish trend in, 61
Tennessee legislature, 25, 68
   Polk in, 23, 31, 32
Tennessee Territory, 17
Texas, 76, 124, 135
   admitted to Union, 100, 136
   as slave state, 132
   see also Republic of Texas
Texas annexation, 76, 93, 94
   Clay's stand against, 97
   in election campaign, 80
   issue of, 8–9, 75–78, 79, 85,
      99–101, 104, 116, 125
Texas revolution, 135, 136, 146
Thirteenth Amendment, 150

Thoreau, Henry David, 145
tight money policies, 31, 57
Tocqueville, Alexis de, 13, 96
Treasury Department, 43
   corruption in, 112
   independent, 1, 60–61
Trist, Nicholas, 151, 152
Truman, Harry, 103, 156
Turney, Hopkins, 62, 114
two-thirds rule, 82, 83
Tyler, John, 4, 63, 104, 105, 112
   nomination for president, 79
   offered Polk cabinet job, 75
   and Polk's presidential
      campaign, 93–94, 99
   Texas annexation issue, 75, 78,
      100
Tyler administration, 61, 104, 122
   and Oregon issue, 123, 125, 127

Union (the), 6, 47
United States Telegraph
   (newspaper), 39, 45, 56
University of North Carolina,
   21–22
Upshur, Abel, 75
U. S. Supreme Court, 24, 129–30

Van Buren, John, 118
Van Buren, Martin, 3, 4, 47, 50,
   58, 69, 72–73, 105, 109, 112
   candidacy, 7, 8, 9, 55, 73–74, 78,
      79–80, 81, 82–84, 85, 153
   cost Polk reelection as governor,
      67–68
   and economy, 59–60
   elected president, 56
   independent Treasury idea, 60,
      61, 102, 122
   met with Clay, 70–72
   organization of power brokers,
      98
   Polk and, 48
   and Polk cabinet, 106–7, 108
   Polk promoting agenda of, 57
   and Polk's presidential
      campaign, 92, 93, 99

Van Buren, Martin (*cont'd*)
  presidential ambitions, 92
  presidential election prospects,
    64
  resigned, 45
  secretary of state, 44–45
  and slavery issue, 77, 85
  and Texas annexation issue,
    71–72, 76–77, 78, 80
  vice president, 51, 54
Van Buren administration, 66
Veracruz, 139, 140
vice presidency, Polk wanted, 3,
  7–8, 66, 66, 68, 69, 72, 73,
  74, 75, 76, 81
Vietnam War, 143, 145
  Gulf of Tonkin incident, 152

Walker, James, 53–54, 62
Walker, Robert, 88–90, 127, 139
  secretary of Treasury, 105, 114,
    147
Wallis, James, 12–13, 16
war(s), 1
  acquisition of California,
    131–50
War Department, 41, 106
Washington, D.C., 39, 132
  politics of, 36, 38
Washington, George, 103
Washington Globe, 45, 50, 51, 76,
  85, 105
  Polk dropped, 112
Washington Union, 112
Webster, Daniel, 29, 52, 55, 56, 75
Webster, Noah, 29
Westcott, James D., 119–20
western lands, 17
Whig administrations, 2
Whig party (Whigs), 4, 7, 20, 71,
  76, 85, 99, 102, 113
  ascendancy, 73–74

attacks on Polk, 152, 156
Clay's presidential campaign,
  91–92, 93, 94, 95, 97
control of Congress, 61
convention in Baltimore, 78, 79
Democrats voting with, 119–20
elected Taylor, 153
gaining momentum, 64
generals were, 133–34, 135, 140
hostility of, 103
in House, 56, 57, 61
and Mexican war, 116, 144,
  146, 152
Polk and, 119
Polk's loss to, 3
and slavery issue, 97, 98
and tariff issue, 90
in Tennessee, 56, 67, 68
won White House, 6
Whig press, 65
White, Hugh Lawson, 32, 39, 50,
  82
  allegation of bribery, 61
  candidacy, 55, 56
  presidential campaign, 61
  unseated, 66
White, Robert, 65, 66
Whitman, Walt, 147
Wickliffe, Charles, 44–45
Williams v. *Norris*, 24
Wilmot, David, 148–49
Wilmot Proviso, 148–50
Wilson, Woodrow, 19, 154
Wise, Henry, 62, 63
Woodbury, Levi, 39, 74, 83, 104
Woodward, George, 129
Wright, Silas, 82, 83, 84–85, 93,
  99, 106, 107

Yancey, William, 25, 26, 31
Yell, Archibald, 137
Young, Brigham, 15